Ethnomusicology: A Very Short Introduction

VERY SHORT INTRODUCTIONS are for anyone wanting a stimulating and accessible way in to a new subject. They are written by experts and have been translated into more than 40 different languages. The series began in 1995 and now covers a wide variety of topics in every discipline. The VSI library contains nearly 400 volumes—a Very Short Introduction to everything from Indian philosophy to psychology and American history—and continues to grow in every subject area.

Very Short Introductions available now:

ADVERTISING Winston Fletcher
AFRICAN HISTORY John Parker and Richard Rathbone
AGNOSTICISM Robin Le Poidevin
AMERICAN HISTORY Paul S. Boyer
AMERICAN IMMIGRATION David A. Gerber
AMERICAN POLITICAL PARTIES AND ELECTIONS L. Sandy Maisel
AMERICAN POLITICS Richard M. Valelly
THE AMERICAN PRESIDENCY Charles O. Jones
ANAESTHESIA Aidan O'Donnell
ANARCHISM Colin Ward
ANCIENT EGYPT Ian Shaw
ANCIENT GREECE Paul Cartledge
THE ANCIENT NEAR EAST Amanda H. Podany
ANCIENT PHILOSOPHY Julia Annas
ANCIENT WARFARE Harry Sidebottom
ANGELS David Albert Jones
ANGLICANISM Mark Chapman
THE ANGLO-SAXON AGE John Blair
THE ANIMAL KINGDOM Peter Holland
ANIMAL RIGHTS David DeGrazia
THE ANTARCTIC Klaus Dodds
ANTISEMITISM Steven Beller
ANXIETY Daniel Freeman and Jason Freeman
THE APOCRYPHAL GOSPELS Paul Foster
ARCHAEOLOGY Paul Bahn
ARCHITECTURE Andrew Ballantyne
ARISTOCRACY William Doyle
ARISTOTLE Jonathan Barnes
ART HISTORY Dana Arnold
ART THEORY Cynthia Freeland
ASTROBIOLOGY David C. Catling
ATHEISM Julian Baggini
AUGUSTINE Henry Chadwick
AUSTRALIA Kenneth Morgan
AUTISM Uta Frith
THE AVANT GARDE David Cottington
THE AZTECS Davíd Carrasco
BACTERIA Sebastian G. B. Amyes
BARTHES Jonathan Culler
THE BEATS David Sterritt
BEAUTY Roger Scruton
BESTSELLERS John Sutherland

THE BIBLE John Riches
BIBLICAL ARCHAEOLOGY Eric H. Cline
BIOGRAPHY Hermione Lee
THE BLUES Elijah Wald
THE BOOK OF MORMON Terryl Givens
BORDERS Alexander C. Diener and Joshua Hagen
THE BRAIN Michael O'Shea
THE BRITISH CONSTITUTION Martin Loughlin
THE BRITISH EMPIRE Ashley Jackson
BRITISH POLITICS Anthony Wright
BUDDHA Michael Carrithers
BUDDHISM Damien Keown
BUDDHIST ETHICS Damien Keown
CANCER Nicholas James
CAPITALISM James Fulcher
CATHOLICISM Gerald O'Collins
CAUSATION Stephen Mumford and Rani Lill Anjum
THE CELL Terence Allen and Graham Cowling
THE CELTS Barry Cunliffe
CHAOS Leonard Smith
CHILDREN'S LITERATURE Kimberley Reynolds
CHINESE LITERATURE Sabina Knight
CHOICE THEORY Michael Allingham
CHRISTIAN ART Beth Williamson
CHRISTIAN ETHICS D. Stephen Long
CHRISTIANITY Linda Woodhead
CITIZENSHIP Richard Bellamy
CIVIL ENGINEERING David Muir Wood
CLASSICAL MYTHOLOGY Helen Morales
CLASSICS Mary Beard and John Henderson
CLAUSEWITZ Michael Howard
CLIMATE Mark Maslin
THE COLD WAR Robert McMahon
COLONIAL AMERICA Alan Taylor
COLONIAL LATIN AMERICAN LITERATURE Rolena Adorno
COMEDY Matthew Bevis
COMMUNISM Leslie Holmes
THE COMPUTER Darrel Ince
THE CONQUISTADORS Matthew Restall and Felipe Fernández-Armesto
CONSCIENCE Paul Strohm
CONSCIOUSNESS Susan Blackmore
CONTEMPORARY ART Julian Stallabrass
CONTEMPORARY FICTION Robert Eaglestone
CONTINENTAL PHILOSOPHY Simon Critchley
COSMOLOGY Peter Coles
CRITICAL THEORY Stephen Eric Bronner
THE CRUSADES Christopher Tyerman
CRYPTOGRAPHY Fred Piper and Sean Murphy
THE CULTURAL REVOLUTION Richard Curt Kraus
DADA AND SURREALISM David Hopkins
DARWIN Jonathan Howard
THE DEAD SEA SCROLLS Timothy Lim
DEMOCRACY Bernard Crick

DERRIDA Simon Glendinning
DESCARTES Tom Sorell
DESERTS Nick Middleton
DESIGN John Heskett
DEVELOPMENTAL BIOLOGY Lewis Wolpert
THE DEVIL Darren Oldridge
DIASPORA Kevin Kenny
DICTIONARIES Lynda Mugglestone
DINOSAURS David Norman
DIPLOMACY Joseph M. Siracusa
DOCUMENTARY FILM Patricia Aufderheide
DREAMING J. Allan Hobson
DRUGS Leslie Iversen
DRUIDS Barry Cunliffe
EARLY MUSIC Thomas Forrest Kelly
THE EARTH Martin Redfern
ECONOMICS Partha Dasgupta
EDUCATION Gary Thomas
EGYPTIAN MYTH Geraldine Pinch
EIGHTEENTH-CENTURY BRITAIN Paul Langford
THE ELEMENTS Philip Ball
EMOTION Dylan Evans
EMPIRE Stephen Howe
ENGELS Terrell Carver
ENGINEERING David Blockley
ENGLISH LITERATURE Jonathan Bate
ENTREPRENEURSHIP Paul Westhead and Mike Wright
ENVIRONMENTAL ECONOMICS Stephen Smith
EPIDEMIOLOGY Rodolfo Saracci
ETHICS Simon Blackburn
ETHNOMUSICOLOGY Timothy Rice
THE EUROPEAN UNION John Pinder and Simon Usherwood
EVOLUTION Brian and Deborah Charlesworth
EXISTENTIALISM Thomas Flynn
FASCISM Kevin Passmore
FASHION Rebecca Arnold
FEMINISM Margaret Walters
FILM Michael Wood
FILM MUSIC Kathryn Kalinak
THE FIRST WORLD WAR Michael Howard
FOLK MUSIC Mark Slobin
FOOD John Krebs
FORENSIC PSYCHOLOGY David Canter
FORENSIC SCIENCE Jim Fraser
FOSSILS Keith Thomson
FOUCAULT Gary Gutting
FRACTALS Kenneth Falconer
FREE SPEECH Nigel Warburton
FREE WILL Thomas Pink
FRENCH LITERATURE John D. Lyons
THE FRENCH REVOLUTION William Doyle
FREUD Anthony Storr
FUNDAMENTALISM Malise Ruthven
GALAXIES John Gribbin
GALILEO Stillman Drake
GAME THEORY Ken Binmore
GANDHI Bhikhu Parekh
GENIUS Andrew Robinson
GEOGRAPHY John Matthews and David Herbert
GEOPOLITICS Klaus Dodds
GERMAN LITERATURE Nicholas Boyle
GERMAN PHILOSOPHY Andrew Bowie
GLOBAL CATASTROPHES Bill McGuire
GLOBAL ECONOMIC HISTORY Robert C. Allen
GLOBAL WARMING Mark Maslin
GLOBALIZATION Manfred Steger

THE GOTHIC Nick Groom
GOVERNANCE Mark Bevir
THE GREAT DEPRESSION AND THE NEW DEAL Eric Rauchway
HABERMAS James Gordon Finlayson
HAPPINESS Daniel M. Haybron
HEGEL Peter Singer
HEIDEGGER Michael Inwood
HERODOTUS Jennifer T. Roberts
HIEROGLYPHS Penelope Wilson
HINDUISM Kim Knott
HISTORY John H. Arnold
THE HISTORY OF ASTRONOMY Michael Hoskin
THE HISTORY OF LIFE Michael Benton
THE HISTORY OF MATHEMATICS Jacqueline Stedall
THE HISTORY OF MEDICINE William Bynum
THE HISTORY OF TIME Leofranc Holford-Strevens
HIV/AIDS Alan Whiteside
HOBBES Richard Tuck
HUMAN EVOLUTION Bernard Wood
HUMAN RIGHTS Andrew Clapham
HUMANISM Stephen Law
HUME A. J. Ayer
IDEOLOGY Michael Freeden
INDIAN PHILOSOPHY Sue Hamilton
INFORMATION Luciano Floridi
INNOVATION Mark Dodgson and David Gann
INTELLIGENCE Ian J. Deary
INTERNATIONAL MIGRATION Khalid Koser
INTERNATIONAL RELATIONS Paul Wilkinson
INTERNATIONAL SECURITY Christopher S. Browning
ISLAM Malise Ruthven
ISLAMIC HISTORY Adam Silverstein
ITALIAN LITERATURE Peter Hainsworth and David Robey
JESUS Richard Bauckham
JOURNALISM Ian Hargreaves
JUDAISM Norman Solomon
JUNG Anthony Stevens
KABBALAH Joseph Dan
KAFKA Ritchie Robertson
KANT Roger Scruton
KEYNES Robert Skidelsky
KIERKEGAARD Patrick Gardiner
THE KORAN Michael Cook
LANDSCAPES AND GEOMORPHOLOGY Andrew Goudie and Heather Viles
LANGUAGES Stephen R. Anderson
LATE ANTIQUITY Gillian Clark
LAW Raymond Wacks
THE LAWS OF THERMODYNAMICS Peter Atkins
LEADERSHIP Keith Grint
LINCOLN Allen C. Guelzo
LINGUISTICS Peter Matthews
LITERARY THEORY Jonathan Culler
LOCKE John Dunn
LOGIC Graham Priest
MACHIAVELLI Quentin Skinner
MADNESS Andrew Scull
MAGIC Owen Davies
MAGNA CARTA Nicholas Vincent
MAGNETISM Stephen Blundell
MALTHUS Donald Winch
MANAGEMENT John Hendry
MAO Delia Davin

MARINE BIOLOGY Philip V. Mladenov
THE MARQUIS DE SADE John Phillips
MARTIN LUTHER Scott H. Hendrix
MARTYRDOM Jolyon Mitchell
MARX Peter Singer
MATHEMATICS Timothy Gowers
THE MEANING OF LIFE Terry Eagleton
MEDICAL ETHICS Tony Hope
MEDICAL LAW Charles Foster
MEDIEVAL BRITAIN John Gillingham and Ralph A. Griffiths
MEMORY Jonathan K. Foster
METAPHYSICS Stephen Mumford
MICHAEL FARADAY Frank A.J.L. James
MODERN ART David Cottington
MODERN CHINA Rana Mitter
MODERN FRANCE Vanessa R. Schwartz
MODERN IRELAND Senia Pašeta
MODERN JAPAN Christopher Goto-Jones
MODERN LATIN AMERICAN LITERATURE Roberto González Echevarría
MODERN WAR Richard English
MODERNISM Christopher Butler
MOLECULES Philip Ball
THE MONGOLS Morris Rossabi
MORMONISM Richard Lyman Bushman
MUHAMMAD Jonathan A.C. Brown
MULTICULTURALISM Ali Rattansi
MUSIC Nicholas Cook
MYTH Robert A. Segal
THE NAPOLEONIC WARS Mike Rapport
NATIONALISM Steven Grosby
NELSON MANDELA Elleke Boehmer
NEOLIBERALISM Manfred Steger and Ravi Roy
NETWORKS Guido Caldarelli and Michele Catanzaro
THE NEW TESTAMENT Luke Timothy Johnson
THE NEW TESTAMENT AS LITERATURE Kyle Keefer
NEWTON Robert Iliffe
NIETZSCHE Michael Tanner
NINETEENTH-CENTURY BRITAIN Christopher Harvie and H. C. G. Matthew
THE NORMAN CONQUEST George Garnett
NORTH AMERICAN INDIANS Theda Perdue and Michael D. Green
NORTHERN IRELAND Marc Mulholland
NOTHING Frank Close
NUCLEAR POWER Maxwell Irvine
NUCLEAR WEAPONS Joseph M. Siracusa
NUMBERS Peter M. Higgins
OBJECTIVITY Stephen Gaukroger
THE OLD TESTAMENT Michael D. Coogan
THE ORCHESTRA D. Kern Holoman
ORGANIZATIONS Mary Jo Hatch
PAGANISM Owen Davies
THE PALESTINIAN-ISRAELI CONFLICT Martin Bunton
PARTICLE PHYSICS Frank Close
PAUL E. P. Sanders
PENTECOSTALISM William K. Kay
THE PERIODIC TABLE Eric R. Scerri
PHILOSOPHY Edward Craig

PHILOSOPHY OF LAW Raymond Wacks
PHILOSOPHY OF SCIENCE Samir Okasha
PHOTOGRAPHY Steve Edwards
PLAGUE Paul Slack
PLANETS David A. Rothery
PLANTS Timothy Walker
PLATO Julia Annas
POLITICAL PHILOSOPHY David Miller
POLITICS Kenneth Minogue
POSTCOLONIALISM Robert Young
POSTMODERNISM Christopher Butler
POSTSTRUCTURALISM Catherine Belsey
PREHISTORY Chris Gosden
PRESOCRATIC PHILOSOPHY Catherine Osborne
PRIVACY Raymond Wacks
PROBABILITY John Haigh
PROGRESSIVISM Walter Nugent
PROTESTANTISM Mark A. Noll
PSYCHIATRY Tom Burns
PSYCHOLOGY Gillian Butler and Freda McManus
PURITANISM Francis J. Bremer
THE QUAKERS Pink Dandelion
QUANTUM THEORY John Polkinghorne
RACISM Ali Rattansi
RADIOACTIVITY Claudio Tuniz
RASTAFARI Ennis B. Edmonds
THE REAGAN REVOLUTION Gil Troy
REALITY Jan Westerhoff
THE REFORMATION Peter Marshall
RELATIVITY Russell Stannard
RELIGION IN AMERICA Timothy Beal
THE RENAISSANCE Jerry Brotton
RENAISSANCE ART Geraldine A. Johnson
RHETORIC Richard Toye
RISK Baruch Fischhoff and John Kadvany
RIVERS Nick Middleton
ROBOTICS Alan Winfield
ROMAN BRITAIN Peter Salway
THE ROMAN EMPIRE Christopher Kelly
THE ROMAN REPUBLIC David M. Gwynn
ROMANTICISM Michael Ferber
ROUSSEAU Robert Wokler
RUSSELL A. C. Grayling
RUSSIAN HISTORY Geoffrey Hosking
RUSSIAN LITERATURE Catriona Kelly
THE RUSSIAN REVOLUTION S. A. Smith
SCHIZOPHRENIA Chris Frith and Eve Johnstone
SCHOPENHAUER Christopher Janaway
SCIENCE AND RELIGION Thomas Dixon
SCIENCE FICTION David Seed
THE SCIENTIFIC REVOLUTION Lawrence M. Principe
SCOTLAND Rab Houston
SEXUALITY Véronique Mottier
SHAKESPEARE Germaine Greer
SIKHISM Eleanor Nesbitt
THE SILK ROAD James A. Millward
SLEEP Steven W. Lockley and Russell G. Foster
SOCIAL AND CULTURAL ANTHROPOLOGY John Monaghan and Peter Just
SOCIALISM Michael Newman

SOCIOLINGUISTICS John Edwards
SOCIOLOGY Steve Bruce
SOCRATES C. C. W. Taylor
THE SOVIET UNION Stephen Lovell
THE SPANISH CIVIL WAR Helen Graham
SPANISH LITERATURE Jo Labanyi
SPINOZA Roger Scruton
SPIRITUALITY Philip Sheldrake
STARS Andrew King
STATISTICS David J. Hand
STEM CELLS Jonathan Slack
STUART BRITAIN John Morrill
SUPERCONDUCTIVITY Stephen Blundell
SYMMETRY Ian Stewart
TERRORISM Charles Townshend
THEOLOGY David F. Ford
THOMAS AQUINAS Fergus Kerr
THOUGHT Tim Bayne
TIBETAN BUDDHISM Matthew T. Kapstein
TOCQUEVILLE Harvey C. Mansfield
TRAGEDY Adrian Poole
THE TROJAN WAR Eric H. Cline
TRUST Katherine Hawley
THE TUDORS John Guy
TWENTIETH-CENTURY BRITAIN Kenneth O. Morgan
THE UNITED NATIONS Jussi M. Hanhimäki
THE U.S. CONGRESS Donald A. Ritchie
THE U.S. SUPREME COURT Linda Greenhouse
UTOPIANISM Lyman Tower Sargent
THE VIKINGS Julian Richards
VIRUSES Dorothy H. Crawford
WITCHCRAFT Malcolm Gaskill
WITTGENSTEIN A. C. Grayling
WORK Stephen Fineman
WORLD MUSIC Philip Bohlman
THE WORLD TRADE ORGANIZATION Amrita Narlikar
WRITING AND SCRIPT Andrew Robinson

Available soon:

BLACK HOLES Katherine Blundell
HUMOUR Noel Carroll
AMERICAN LEGAL HISTORY G. Edward White
REVOLUTIONS Jack A. Goldstone
FAMILY LAW Jonathan Herring

For more information visit our web site

www.oup.co.uk/general/vsi/

Timothy Rice

ETHNOMUSICOLOGY

A Very Short Introduction

OXFORD
UNIVERSITY PRESS

Oxford University Press is a department of the University of Oxford.
It furthers the University's objective of excellence in research,
scholarship, and education by publishing worldwide.

Oxford New York
Auckland Cape Town Dar es Salaam Hong Kong Karachi
Kuala Lumpur Madrid Melbourne Mexico City Nairobi
New Delhi Shanghai Taipei Toronto

With offices in
Argentina Austria Brazil Chile Czech Republic France Greece
Guatemala Hungary Italy Japan Poland Portugal Singapore
South Korea Switzerland Thailand Turkey Ukraine Vietnam

Published in the United States of America by
Oxford University Press
198 Madison Avenue, New York, NY 10016

Library of Congress Cataloging-in-Publication Data
Rice, Timothy, 1945–
Ethnomusicology : a very short introduction / Timothy Rice.
pages cm.—(Very short introductions)
Includes bibliographical references and index.
ISBN 978-0-19-979437-9 (alk. paper)
1. Ethnomusicology. I. Title.
ML3798.R53 2014
780.89—dc23 2013020199

Printed in Great Britain
by Ashford Colour Press Ltd., Gosport, Hants.
on acid-free paper

Contents

List of illustrations xiii

Acknowledgments xv

1 Defining ethnomusicology 1

2 A bit of history 11

3 Conducting research 27

4 The nature of music 44

5 Music as culture 65

6 Individual musicians 79

7 Writing music history 88

8 Ethnomusicology in the modern world 98

9 Ethnomusicologists at work 113

References 123

Further reading 135

Listening 141

Index 145

List of illustrations

1 Béla Bartók recording villagers on a wax-cylinder phonograph **16**
Photo by Gyula Kósa, 1907, courtesy of the Bartók Archive, Hungarian Academy of Sciences, and Gábor Vásárhely

2 Anne Rasmussen performs with Indonesian Qur'anic reciters **36**
Courtesy of Anne Rasmussen, 2004

3 Simha Arom playing back recordings for Aka musicians **39**
Photograph by Harald Schmitt, 2001

4 Mantle Hood illustrates the playing of the Javanese *rebab* **52**
Photographer unknown, ca. 1959, courtesy of the UCLA Ethnomusicology Archive. © The Regents of the University of California, All Rights Reserved

5 North Indian vocalist Ustad Yunus Husain Khan and accompanists **55**
Photograph by Daniel Neuman, ca. 1991

6 Anthony Seeger dancing with the Suyá **70**
Photograph by Judith Seeger, 1972

7 Professional Bulgarian bagpipe (*gaida*) player Kostadin Varimezov **83**
Photograph by Vergilii Atanasov, 1980s

8 Ming Dynasty manuscript with drawings of musical instruments **90**
Courtesy of Joseph S. C. Lam

9 Protestant band with fifes and Lambeg drums **109**
Courtesy of Hugo and Ray Weir

10 Daniel Sheehy at the Smithsonian Folklife Festival in 2009 **118**
Courtesy of the Smithsonian Institution

List of Illustrations

Acknowledgments

Even a very short book like this one has required the help of many people. It is my pleasure to acknowledge their assistance here. I would like to thank Nancy Toff at Oxford University Press for entrusting me with this task, and her colleague Suzanne Ryan for referring me to her. Two graduate students at UCLA provided essential research assistance, Chloe Coventry and Katie Stuffelbeam. Graduate students Jeffrey van den Scott at Northwestern University and Svend Kjeldsen at the University of Limerick read through two earlier versions of the manuscript and provided insightful comments. A number of former students reviewed a draft and saved me from some infelicities of content and style: Michael Bakan, Leslie Hall, Jonathan Ritter, and Louise Wrazen. I am especially grateful to four colleagues who agreed to pilot the book in their graduate seminars: Timothy Cooley at University of California, Santa Barbara, Inna Naroditskaya at Northwestern University, Colin Quigley at the University of Limerick, and Deborah Wong at University of California, Riverside. Their students' comments helped me in many ways including fathoming the range of readers for a book like this, not least their parents. Finally, I am exceedingly grateful to Kathleen Rice, my PhD-toting cousin, for her extraordinarily perspicacious copyediting of a previous draft.

I have relied on many colleagues to help me find, and provide me with, the photographs that appear in this book. Those whose photos appear in the book are listed, and I thank them for their willingness to allow me to use them. I would also like to acknowledge the help, in this regard, of a number of others: Lars-Christian Koch at the Berliner Phongramm-Archiv; Todd Harvey at the American Folklife Center, Library of Congress; Vikárius László and Büky Virág at the Bartók Archives of the Hungarian Academy of Sciences, and Gábor Vásárhely, heir to the Bartók estate; Dianne Thram at the International Library of African Music; Stephanie Smith from the Smithsonian Institution; Aaron Bittel and Maureen Russell at the UCLA Ethnomusicology Archive; Gregory Barz; Paul Berliner; David Cooper; Steven Feld; Katherine Hagedorn; Ellen Koskoff; Barbara and A. J. Racy; Sonia Seeman; Zoe Sherinian; and Kathleen Van Buren.

Chapter 1
Defining ethnomusicology

Ethnomusicology is the study of why, and how, human beings are musical. This definition positions ethnomusicology among the social sciences, humanities, and biological sciences dedicated to understanding the nature of the human species in all its biological, social, cultural, and artistic diversity.

"Musical" in this definition does not refer to musical talent or ability; rather it refers to the capacity of humans to create, perform, organize cognitively, react physically and emotionally to, and interpret the meanings of humanly organized sounds. The definition assumes that all humans, not just those we call musicians, are musical to some degree, and that musicality (the capacity to make and make sense of music) defines our humanity and provides one of the touchstones of human experience. Musical thinking and doing may be as important to our human being in the world as is our ability to speak and to understand speech. Ethnomusicologists would claim we need music to be fully human.

Ethnomusicologists believe that to understand our humanity through our musicality, that is, to understand why we need music to be fully human, we must study music in all its diversity. The basic question, why and how are humans musical, will not be answered by studying a small slice of the world's music. All music, in its full geographical and historical extent, must be studied. Ethnomusicologists do not begin their research with a judgment about what they imagine is "good music" or "music worthy of study" or "music that has withstood the test of time." Instead, they assume that whenever and wherever humans make and listen to music with the keen devotion and attention that they do, then something important and worthy of study is going on.

So another definition might state that ethnomusicology is the study of all of the world's music. Although this definition tells us what ethnomusicologists study, it does not explain why they cast their net so widely. They do so because they want to answer big questions about the nature of music and the nature of humankind. The British ethnomusicologist John Blacking (1928–90), in his book *How Musical Is Man?*, to which my opening definition is partially indebted, captures this ethnomusicological sensibility this way:

> In this world of cruelty and exploitation . . . it is necessary to understand why a madrigal by Gesualdo or a Bach Passion, a *sitar* melody from India or a song from Africa, Berg's *Wozzeck* or Britten's *War Requiem*, a Balinese *gamelan* or a Cantonese opera, or a symphony by Mozart, Beethoven, or Mahler may be profoundly necessary for human survival, quite apart from any merit they may have as examples of creativity and technical progress. It is also necessary to explain why, under certain circumstances, a "simple" "folk" song may have more human value than a "complex" symphony.

These opening definitions imply the study of the music of all the world's peoples as a path to understanding human beings. Other ways to define the field emanate from unpacking the word "ethnomusicology" into its three Greek roots: *ethnos*, *mousikē*, and *logos*.

Ethnos

In ancient Greek *ethnos* referred to people of the same nation, tribe, or race. It is the root of such phrases as ethnic group, ethnic minority, and ethnic music. Its inclusion in the term "ethnomusicology" suggests that ethnomusicology might be defined as the study (*logos*) of the music (*mousikē*) of groups of people (*ethnos*), especially those sharing a common language and culture—ethnic groups in other words. That was undoubtedly part of the original conception of the field when the Dutch musicologist Jaap Kunst (1891–1960) first published the word "ethno-musicology" in 1950 in a small book called *Musicologia: A Study of the Nature of Ethno-musicology, Its Problems, Methods, and Representative Personalities.* In creating the name, Kunst combined the names of two older disciplines, musicology (created in 1885) and ethnology (often dated to 1783). Musicology is the study of music. Ethnology is the comparative study of human linguistic and cultural diversity based on direct contact with, and ethnographic accounts of, particular groups of people. Ethnomusicology, by extension, was to be the comparative study of human musical diversity based on musical ethnography.

This alternate definition has the advantage of adding the principal method ethnomusicologists use to study why and how human beings are musical, namely, the ethnographic, or fieldwork, method. Applying this method to particular cultures and societies has yielded thousands of studies of the extent to which music is governed by, and affects, deep cultural principles and social structures. The extensive application of the ethnographic method in myriad intensive studies has moved the field away from the comparative impulse inherent in the term "ethnology" and toward the definition of the field as the study of music in (or as) culture and to studies that posit something called a "music culture." In 1960 Alan Merriam (1923–80), one of the seminal figures in the field, defined ethnomusicology in just this way: "[T]he study of music in culture"; but a sentence or two later he returned the definition of the field to the universality implied in my opening definition: "[T]he study of music as a universal aspect of man's activities." The two poles of the culturally particular and the humanly universal, whether understood as a tension or productive antitheses, have galvanized ethnomusicologists' thinking about their field ever since.

The interest, inherent in the name of the field, in music making by groups of people has also broadened over the years. While the majority of ethnomusicological studies continue to focus on music making within a culture or society traditionally understood as a national or ethnic group, modern life is causing many societies and cultures to fragment and recombine. Individuals find it advantageous, and in some cases necessary, to escape their social and cultural roots, move to new places, and connect with, or even create, new social groups. These new social groups sometimes have their basis in ethnicity. Just as often modern conditions invite individuals to create "subcultural" or "microcultural" groups based on shared work, class, recreational experiences, or affinity for surfing, sci-fi movies, or flamenco music. Hence, the simple definition I started with does not emphasize the study of why, and how, human *groups* are musical, as the name of the discipline implies, but how and why humans, individually and in any of the many ways they congregate, are musical. This caveat has led some to argue that the very name of the field is no longer appropriate and should be abandoned.

Mousikē

The Greek word *mousikē*, in the form of the English word "music," has come to refer to the art of organizing sound in pleasing or thought-provoking ways. As ethnomusicologists have studied musical diversity around the world, however, that simple definition of music has proven problematic.

Music is not an easy word to define, partly because its meanings expanded considerably in the second half of the twentieth century.

Whereas music may once have been defined as pleasing sounds organized around such reliable elements as melody, harmony, and rhythm, some modern music has added to or subtracted from these elements in ways that challenge any simple understanding of what music might be. Rap music, for example, substitutes rhythmic declamation of lyrics for singing them to a tune, leaving some uninitiated listeners mystified as to whether it is "really" music. The American composer John Cage (1912–92) famously composed a piece called *4′33″* (1952) that directed the pianist to sit at the keyboard for that length of time without playing a note. Even the notion that music should be "humanly organized sound," a definition proposed by John Blacking, may be too limited. Cage and others sought to create music in which the organization was left to chance rather than human agency. In another twist, English speakers frequently, if metaphorically, speak of bird and whale "song." Are the organized sounds of animals music? These challenges to the definition of music within Euro-American culture mirror similar challenges in the cultures ethnomusicologists study.

Ethnomusicologists have learned, for example, that in agricultural and pastoral cultures, where people work outdoors most of the time, humans sometimes sing in counterpoint with the sounds of animals and the natural environment, as if animals and nature were singing to and with us. Does this mean that our definition of music as humanly organized sound is too narrow? Because all humans live in and interact with sounding environments, whether the sounds of nature or the sounds of modern warfare, some ethnomusicologists have begun to suggest recently that our object of study should be that of sound and not just of music. That view challenges our simple definition of the field. Perhaps someday ethnomusicologists will have created an "ethnosonicology."

The boundary that my first definition implicitly erects between music and other performing arts, such as dance, poetry, or theater, is not universal. In parts of Bantu-speaking East Africa, for example, the word for drum, *ngoma*, has been extended to include singing, dancing, hand-clapping, and ululating on social occasions. There seems to be no term quite comparable to "music" in English. In other cultures the word music applies to a narrower range of musical behaviors than in the West. In some strict interpretations of Islam, for example, music and singing refer only to secular practices and have a distinctly negative connotation, whereas the musical qualities of sacred expressions are labeled "chanting" or "reciting" and have positive associations. In Bulgaria, where I conducted my ethnomusicological field studies, villagers used the term "music" (*muzika*) to refer only to instrumental music. Other modes of what I would consider musical expression, such as singing, drumming, and lamenting, had different names and were considered distinct from music.

Another problem with the term "music" is that it refers to a product rather than a process. As a result, early studies in the field of ethnomusicology often focused on elements and structures of music that had been fixed in musical notation or in sound recordings. Such studies did not capture what ethnomusicologists observed during their fieldwork, namely the interactions between all the human beings present during a musical event, the motivations behind their behaviors, and the significance they attach to them.

To capture the intellectual, physical, cultural, and social dynamics and processes that generate musical products, we need a locution with a verbal rather than a nominal form. One might be "to make music," giving us ethnomusicology as the study of how and why people make music, or more simply, the study of people making music, a definition advanced by Jeff Todd Titon. This definition works if we understand "making music" to include not only the playing of music but also how humans "make" music perceptually, conceptually, and emotionally as well.

The music educator Christopher Small (1927–2011) provided another solution in a book titled *Musicking*. By transforming the noun "music" into a new verb, "to music," he redefined music as an activity rather than a thing. He wanted this neologism to capture all the musical thinking, the "musicking," humans do—not just playing music but responding and assigning meanings to the musical sounds made by others. To capture this sense of music as activity, I settled on the verb phrase "are musical" in my opening definition. Echoing John Blacking's title, *How Musical is Man?*, this definition avoids the inconvenient noun music and the yet-not-widely-used verb "to music," and implies an interest in all the ways humans are musical as they make, perceive, interpret, and respond in myriad ways to sound.

Beyond the vexing questions of what is music and whether to refer to it as a product or a process, there is the question of what kinds of music ethnomusicologists study. If the goal of the field is to understand human musicking, or how and why humans are musical, then the answer must be that ethnomusicologists study all music. However, the first published definition of the field, by Jaap Kunst in 1950, limited its scope:

> The study-object of ethnomusicology, or as it was originally called: comparative musicology, is the traditional music and musical instruments of all cultural strata of mankind, from the so-called primitive peoples to the civilized nations. Our science, therefore, investigates all tribal and folk music and every kind of non-European art music. . . . European art- and popular (entertainment-) music do not belong to its field.

Because most ethnomusicologists believe they should study music as a universal human phenomenon, it makes no sense to exclude some part of that phenomenon, as Kunst's original definition did. And yet, as a practical matter, the vast majority of ethnomusicological research and teaching today concerns what have been variously called—and few ethnomusicologists are happy with these terms—"traditional music," "non-Western music," or "world music." (World music, in the ethnomusicological sense, is a category far broader than the use of the phrase, since the late 1980s, to denote commercial and popular "ethno-pop" musical fusions.) While popular music from most parts of the world, as well as American "ethnic" forms of popular music, are now well-accepted "study-objects," studies of European classical music and Anglo-American popular music, with some important exceptions, remain rather thin on the ground.

This definition—ethnomusicology is the study of traditional forms of non-Western or world music—has some advantages. It is easy for nonspecialists to understand, and it is an accurate description, within limits, of what ethnomusicologists actually do. Ethnomusicologists tend to use it when family and friends ask what "ethnomusicology" is. But it is not a very popular definition within the field, because it places the West in the center and marginalizes the rest, arguably the vast majority of human beings. This definition also fails to explain why we conduct these studies, and it obfuscates the larger goals of the enterprise captured in my opening definition.

Logos

In Greek the word *logos* means, among other things, "word," "reason," "logic," "discourse," and, in the form of the suffix "-ology," it has been adopted for many disciplinary names in English. Hence, ethnomusicology is word-based, reasoned discourse about music. This definition does not distinguish ethnomusicology from other forms of musicology, such as the study of European art music. However, it does set up a dichotomy between ethnomusicological study, which results in reports in the spoken and written word, and other forms of "studying music," such as taking music lessons and learning to play and compose music. Because ethnomusicology is sometimes defined as the study of "world music," some musicians who learn and perform music beyond the realms of Euro-American art and popular music call themselves ethnomusicologists. Historically this appropriation of the term "ethnomusicologist" by performers and their critics has caused some consternation among academic ethnomusicologists. Today, the general attitude seems more relaxed. The website of the U.S.-based Society for Ethnomusicology takes an ecumenical view and welcomes not only scholars to become members but also performers. As a matter of method, during their fieldwork with musicians, ethnomusicologists ask questions about how various musicians make and think about music, inviting them to provide "reasoned discourse" and, in effect, to become musicologists. Still, it would probably be fair to define ethnomusicology as an academic discipline based on reasoned discourse in words about the full range, in all places and time periods, of human music making.

Defining ethnomusicology is not a simple matter. The definition I started with proliferated. Each one tells us something slightly different about what people who call themselves ethnomusicologists do, and each is useful as a tactic for specifying the intellectual goals of the field, its subject matter, its methods and actual practices, or its differences from other fields.

Ethnomusicology is the study of why, and how, human beings are musical.
Ethnomusicology is the study of all of the world's music.
Ethnomusicology is the study of groups of people making music.
Ethnomusicology is the comparative study of human musical diversity based on fieldwork and musical ethnography.
Ethnomusicology is the study of traditional, non-Western, or world music.
Ethnomusicology is the study of music in (or as) culture.
Ethnomusicology is the study of humanly organized sound.
Ethnomusicology is the study of music and the sound environments in which it is made.
Ethnomusicology is the study of people making music.
Ethnomusicology is the study of human musicking.

Ethnomusicology is word-based, reasoned discourse about all music.

Ethnomusicology is the study of world music by any means, verbal and nonverbal.

Ethnomusicology is an academic discipline based on reasoned discourse in words about the full range, in all places and time periods, of human music and music making.

The remainder of this very short introduction looks in more detail at how ethnomusicologists have studied the diversity of human musicality, including the history of the field, its methods, principal insights, and the contexts in which it is practiced.

Chapter 2
A bit of history

The ethnomusicological interest in understanding why and how humans are musical clearly has its roots in older ways of thinking about music.

Ancient and medieval precursors

The ancient literate cultures of China and Greece generated philosophical treatises on music because they believed, like modern ethnomusicologists, that music is an extraordinarily important cultural expression with deep cosmological, metaphysical, religious, social, and political implications. Early Greek thinking about music, often personified by Pythagoras (ca. 570–ca. 490 BCE), held that the cosmos and the key to wisdom were governed by ratios of small whole numbers. Once the Greeks demonstrated that musical intervals such as the octave, perfect fifth, and perfect fourth could be explained by ratios of small whole numbers, they concluded that music must be an important cog in the moral universe and the cosmological "harmony of the spheres." This view is expressed in many variants in the nonliterate cultures ethnomusicologists have studied.

The ethnomusicological literature is filled with arguments that echo the ancient Greeks about whether music helps to construct behavioral, cultural, and psychological patterns or whether preexisting social structures and cultural systems are determinants of musical style and practice. Plato (ca. 429–347 BCE), for example, wrote, in the *Republic* and elsewhere, that music affected ethical behavior and therefore the political life of a society. He associated the stereotypical ethical qualities of the various Greek subgroups (Phrygians, Ionians, Dorians) with the musical modes (the set of intervals between tones in a scale) they played on their lutes and lyres, and he concluded that playing those modes caused those behaviors, some good and some bad. Thus political leaders, "philosopher-kings," would be justified in banning certain modes because of their adverse effect on people.

In China, at about the same time, many treatises spoke about the fundamental nature of music in human life. The Chinese sage Confucius (551–479 BCE) was believed to have been a practicing musician. He thought that training in "proper" music, the kind played during rituals, could cultivate good qualities in the ruling class and thus in the state itself, while entertainment music would have the opposite effect. The Chinese were the first to create the idea of fixed pitch, that is, the setting of a pitch to a particular number of vibrations per second (in the West, for example, the idea that the pitch A equals 440 cycles per second). The melodies using these fixed pitches were believed to be so fundamental to political and social functioning that when a new dynasty took power, it would reset the fixed pitches of music to new levels.

In the early Middle Ages, Saint Augustine (354–430) believed that musical performance (*musica sonora*) was a way for humankind to reach beyond the mundane to contemplate divinity. The Roman writer Boethius (480–524) elucidated Greek ideas about music in his five-volume *De institutione musica*, including the idea that musical performance had ethical implications. Ethnomusicologists today are familiar with both views.

In India, between the fourth and thirteenth centuries, various forms of practice and knowledge (medicine, theater, and music) needed to be legitimated by logically constructed doctrines and reasoned discourse. The resulting treatises speculate on metaphysical ideas about the sources of creative energy in vibration and the affective link between melodic modes and their use in theatrical scenes to accompany certain moods or actions.

In the Middle East, from the seventh to the thirteenth centuries, important works on music appeared in Arabic. Inspired by reading ancient Greek literature, scholars made music a central topic in their encyclopedias and other works. Abū Naṣr al-Fārābī (872–951) wrote an important treatise on music theory called *Kitāb al-mūsīqī al-kabīr* ("The Great Book of Music"). Abū al-Faraj al-Iṣbahānī (897–967) compiled the *Kitāb al-aghānī* ("Book of Songs"), a twenty-four-volume work on the musical practices of the day. It included anecdotes about musical events and the social and cultural practices guiding performances of music, accounts that anticipate contemporary ethnomusicological studies.

Exploration and enlightenment

The scholars of the ancient and medieval worlds, with a few exceptions, commented on their own musical traditions. This situation changed with the age of exploration and the opening up of the New World to European colonization. In Latin America Jesuit missionaries, as early as the sixteenth century, studied the music of the indigenous people they found there for the purpose of converting them to Christianity. Today's ethnomusicology, at least that branch of it that has ethnomusicologists from North America, Europe, Australia, New Zealand, and Japan traveling the globe to study the music of other people, has some of its roots in colonialism and imperialism. Sir William Jones (1746–94), an English colonial judge in the Supreme Court in Calcutta, may have been the first European to write about India's classical music.

European interest in the music of others was also stimulated in eighteenth-century France by the Enlightenment, which was about, among other things, the acquisition of universal knowledge unfettered by dogma and tradition. Works in this vein include Jean-Jacques Rousseau's (1712–78) *Dictionnaire de musique*, which provided notations of Native American and Chinese music, and Jean Joseph Marie Amiot's (1718–93) *Mémoire sur la musique des Chinois*. Another example in this spirit was the work of the Englishman Charles Burney (1726–1814), a pioneer of historical musicology who traveled to the Continent and wrote a number of books that might be considered, in today's terms, ethnographies of musical life there.

Nationalism, musical folklore, and ethnology

The Enlightenment interest in music of the Other was paralleled by the rise of Romantic nationalism. Nationalism, the belief that each ethnic group (called under this doctrine a "nationality") has a right to its own state, arose in Europe in the late eighteenth century and became arguably the dominant political ideology of the nineteenth century. In the nineteenth and twentieth centuries the Austro-Hungarian, Ottoman, and Russian Empires, the latter succeeded by the former Soviet Union, dissolved into nation-states, while many of the city-states and principalities of central and southern Europe became the nation-states of Germany and Italy. To help create the idea of nation and the cultural life of new nation-states, there arose the view, first promulgated by Johann Gottfried von Herder (1744–1803), that national identity and spirit was most authentically expressed in rural speech, folktales, and folksong lyrics and melodies. To support the search for a nation's patrimony, "musical folklorists" began to collect "folk songs" from peasant villagers in the countryside. Transcriptions of these songs in musical notation were compiled in books that took their place alongside the ostensibly great works of literature and art music in the nation's libraries. Classically trained composers, often the collectors themselves, used the peasants' melodies to write "national music," typically orchestral tone poems, rhapsodies, and operas that expressed the national spirit for an urban bourgeois audience. This political impetus to study the music of ourselves generated enormous amounts of valuable scholarship on rural musical traditions under threat from urbanization, education, and industrialization.

Each nation had its indefatigable collectors and activists, among the most famous of whom were Cecil Sharp (1859–1924), Ralph Vaughan Williams (1872–1958), and Percy Grainger (1882–1961) in England; Nikolay Rimsky-Korsakov (1844–1908) in Russia; and Béla Bartók (1881–1945) and Zoltán Kodály (1882–1967) in Hungary. In 1947 the need for international cooperation, manifested in the creation of the United Nations, had its parallel in European folklorists' creation of the International Folk Music Council (IFMC), a UNESCO-affiliated organization, with Ralph Vaughn Williams as its first president. In the 1960s, as new states in Africa and elsewhere threw off imperial domination, the impetus to study national forms of music spread to nearly every corner of the world and to genres of music not properly understood as "folk." In 1981 the IFMC changed its name to the International Council for Traditional Music (ICTM), and it continues to flourish today as an important institution supporting an international dialogue among scholars studying primarily the music of their own nations.

In the United States the impetus to collect traditional music was linked not to nationalism but to ethnological studies of Native Americans. Alice Cunningham Fletcher (1838–1923), trained in ethnology at the Peabody Museum at Harvard University, began fieldwork among the Lakota in 1881 and published more than forty monographs, many with descriptions of songs, dances, games, and stories. Frances Densmore (1867–1957), trained in music at Oberlin College, made many recordings on wax cylinders for the Bureau of American Ethnology and published books on a host of tribal musical traditions.

1. Béla Bartók records villagers in Darázs (Dražovce in present-day Slovakia) on a wax-cylinder phonograph in 1907.

Comparative musicology

In nineteenth-century Europe the rise of nationalism and its concern with the music of a national self overshadowed the Enlightenment and colonialist fascination with music of the Other. However, those preoccupations were relaunched in the late nineteenth century when the Austrian scholar Guido Adler (1855–1941) published his 1885 outline of a new field of study called *Musikwissenschaft*, musical science or, in English, musicology. Arguing that its purpose was the "discovery of the true and advancement of the beautiful," he divided musicology into two main branches, historical and systematic. The first was concerned primarily with the history of European art music. The systematic branch, on the other hand, was divided into a plethora of subfields, including music theory, pedagogy, aesthetics, and comparative musicology. In this conception, comparative musicology and historical musicology were subfields of a broadly conceived musicology. Since that time the term "musicology" has come to refer, principally though not exclusively, to the historical study of European art music. Ethnomusicology is no longer one of its subfields.

Comparative musicologists, many trained in psychology, were musical ethnologists. In 1886 Carl Stumpf (1848–1936), a psychologist and philosopher, wrote one of the first musical ethnographies on the Bella Coola Indians of British Columbia, who had been invited to travel to Berlin and twenty-one other European cities in 1885. Today comparative musicologists are principally remembered for comparing data provided in accounts of local musical practices by missionaries, diplomats, and travelers. Their work was aided immensely by—and indeed the field of ethnomusicology depends on—the invention of the phonograph in 1877. (The earliest recordings of "world music" are usually attributed to Walter Fewkes [1850–1930], an American anthropologist who, in 1890, made the first recordings of Native American music.) Their comparisons focused on five principal issues: (1) the origins of music; (2) musical evolution; (3) understanding the distribution of musical styles and artifacts around the world; (4) musical style analysis and comparison; and (5) the classification and measurement of musical phenomena such as pitch, scales, and musical instruments. They assumed, for example, that what they called "primitive music" was a survival of humankind's earliest music, and so it could be used to answer the question of music's origins. Studies of musical evolution, whose authors were influenced by the social Darwinism of Herbert Spencer (1820–1903), tried to demonstrate how musical elements such as scales and modes, rhythms, harmonies, forms, and musical instruments evolved from simple to complex, from a few tones in a scale to many, and from a single line of melody to multipart polyphony. They imagined a universal music history culminating in European art music.

Comparative musicologists argued about whether the distribution of similar musical features and instruments around the world was due to monogenesis, that is, their invention in one place followed by their distribution to many places, or to polygenesis, that is, their invention in many places. One theory, borrowed from German ethnologists of the period and known as "culture-circle theory," used distribution studies to claim that the more widespread a form was, the older it was. So, for example, the wider distribution around the world of end-blown whistle flutes, like the recorder, compared to the transverse flute was taken as evidence that whistle flutes were a more ancient instrument type than the transverse flute. Their musical style analysis and comparison reduced dynamic, temporal musical processes to a fixed product made up of "elements" such as melody, rhythm, texture, and form. While European musical folklorists were subjecting their own traditions to this sort of analysis in order to discover the nature of their particular national musical style or its regional variants or dialects, comparative musicologists were doing the same for musical styles around the world.

Because they were studying musical phenomena in all its global variety, comparative musicologists needed a way to write about them that would transcend the categories and classifications of European music. They needed, in other words, comparative methods. The two most influential and enduring projects were a system for comparing pitch intervals and a system for classifying musical instruments. Ethnomusicologists still use both of them today.

The interval-comparison technique, called the "cents" system, was invented in the 1880s by the English philologist and mathematician Alexander John Ellis (1814–90). The cents system was designed to overcome the problem of comparing pitch intervals using the ratio of frequencies of each pitch. When the numbers are small, comparing the sizes of intervals is relatively easy: 2:1 is obviously greater than 3:2. When the numbers become much larger, comparison of what are geometrical relationships becomes very difficult. So Ellis employed a logarithmic function to transform the geometric ratios of frequencies to an easily understood arithmetic scale. He divided the octave into 1,200 units so that each equal-tempered half-step was 100 units or "cents." Comparing music from all over the world with this new tool, Ellis discovered that tuning systems were far too varied to be explained by a mathematical theory such as numerical ratios or a natural phenomenon such as the harmonic series, the complex set of pitches that sound when a musical tone is sung or played. His new measuring tool allowed him to contradict Pythagoras and all the others after him who claimed that musical scales can be explained mathematically or naturally as opposed to culturally. Although Ellis did not employ a theory of culture, he demonstrated that musical scales are "very diverse, very artificial, and very capricious." They must result from human intervention and choice rather than from nature, a position modern ethnomusicologists share.

The ability to compare things is greatly aided by systematic analytical methods and classificatory frameworks into which particular instances can be placed. Simple examples in music theory include melodic modes, which can be classified by the number of tones in the octave (pentatonic, heptatonic, octatonic) and meters (duple, triple, additive). Ethnomusicologists routinely use these sorts of schemes to talk about music. Comparative musicologists elaborated them to a great extent, and one that continues to be used today is a system for the classification of musical instruments created by Curt Sachs (1881–1959) and Erich von Hornbostel (1877–1935) in Berlin, and published in 1914. Known as the Sachs-Hornbostel system, it divides musical instruments into four groups according to the primary vibrating material: air (aerophones), string (chordophones), skin (membranophones), and solids (idiophones). Each major class was further subdivided in ways appropriate to it: aerophones by the method of "excitation" (flutes, reeds, and horns); chordophones by the geometry of the neck and body (lutes, harps, zithers, and lyres); membranophones by the shape of the resonator (barrel, cylinder, kettle, vase, hourglass); and idiophones by the material (wood, stone, metal). Originally designed so that instruments in museum collections could be cataloged like books, the system remains in use among ethnomusicologists, who prefer to call an instrument from another culture either by its actual name, say bouzoukee, or by its Sachs-Hornbostel classificatory description, "long-necked, fretted, pear-shaped, plucked lute," rather than using an ethnocentric culture-to-culture comparison like "Greek guitar."

The impulse to study music beyond one's own borders was not limited during this period to Europeans. In Japan Kishibe Shigeo (1912–2005) and his colleagues established a Society (and journal) for Research in Asiatic Music in 1936, and in 1945 scholars in Chile founded *Revista musical chilena*, dedicated to the study of Chilean and Latin American music.

Early ethnomusicology

Research in comparative musicology faded for obvious reasons during World War II. When Jaap Kunst suggested a new name for the enterprise after the war, it caught on immediately, especially in the United States. The combination of anthropological and musicological study in the new disciplinary name captured the imagination of a group of four American anthropologists and musicologists: Charles Seeger (1886–1979), Willard Rhodes (1901–92), David McAllester (1916–2006), and Alan Merriam. In 1953 they started an *Ethno-musicology Newsletter*, established the Society for Ethno-Musicology in 1954, held their first annual meeting in 1956, and transformed the newsletter into the journal *Ethnomusicology* in 1958. By the early 1960s the first graduate programs in this newly named field had sprouted in anthropology at Indiana University and in music at the University of California, Los Angeles and the University of Illinois at Urbana-Champaign. Since then this discipline with the awkward name has continued to grow in institutional and intellectual clout to the present day.

The name change from comparative musicology to ethnomusicology initiated a gradual decline in the salience of the musicological problems that characterized the older field. Instead, the new discipline moved in the direction of studies of "music as culture." Such studies view music as a human activity linked to other aspects of culture such as religion, art, language, politics, dance, crafts, and social institutions. The new discipline, with its roots in musicology and anthropology, suggested new questions that the older discipline had not asked. Why do people in particular places sing and play and dance the way they do? To what purposes has humankind put music? If music making can be regarded as a social behavior as well as an artistic behavior, then how is it embedded within societies and their social structures? Is musical behavior consistent or coherent with other social behaviors and cultural patterns, or does it challenge them in some way? What social and cultural issues are at stake in the teaching and learning of music? Can music and its constituent elements have culturally shared meanings associated with them and, if so, what are those meanings? This new discipline captured the spirit of the long history, going back to the ancient Chinese and Greeks, of scholarly fascination with music's significance in human life.

When the word "ethnomusicology" burst on the scene in the 1950s, it completely erased the name "comparative musicology," and along with it that discipline's grand theories of musical origins, universal music history, musical evolution, and culture-circle distribution of musical traits. Although some early ethnomusicologists argued against comparison in favor of more detailed ethnographic work in particular cultures, comparative musical analysis and the scientific impulse that drove it did not immediately subside. Bruno Nettl, in his 1954 *North American Indian Musical Styles*, analyzed structural similarities and differences between the music of neighboring tribes in order to create a classification of regional musical styles. Mieczyslaw Kolinski (1901–81), born in Poland and an immigrant to the United States and Canada, invented an extraordinarily elaborate system to classify melodic shapes in the 1960s. In 1971 Mantle Hood (1918–2005), founder of the ethnomusicology program at UCLA, published a comparative tool he called "hardness scales" so that ethnomusicologists could compare maximum and minimum ranges of such musical features as loudness, pitch, timbre, and density (pulse per minute).

The continued interest in musicological analysis was also reflected in an efflorescence of articles in the new journal *Ethnomusicology* on how to transcribe musical sound into musical notation, and on the problem of a transcription's reliability (would two people transcribing the same piece get the same results) and validity (can European notation accurately reflect the melodic and rhythmic complexities of the music created in aural traditions). A "symposium," published in 1964 and edited by Nicholas England (1922–2003), featured four prominent ethnomusicologists' transcriptions of a song performed by a Bushman from southern Africa to the accompaniment of a musical bow. The striking differences among them were signs of the unreliability of the exercise. These concerns about the reliability and validity of musical notation are no longer as important as they were when comparison of musical structures recorded in musical notation was a core problem of early ethnomusicology. The problems of transcription were pushed into the background as ethnomusicologists renounced comparative musicological studies in favor of more in-depth, fieldwork-based idiographic studies of "musical cultures."

Although musicological analysis was never completely abandoned, the anthropological study of musical cultures was sparked to a large degree when, in 1964, Alan Merriam published *The Anthropology of Music*. Merriam argued that the study of the "music sound itself" was but one "analytical level" in the ethnomusicological study of "music in culture." In other words, the "ethno" part of ethnomusicology required two other analytical levels, "conceptualization about music [and] behavior in relation to music," levels that had not been worked out at that time in the same detail as musicological analysis and comparison had been. Apart from this three-part model of ethnomusicological analysis, Merriam's most important contribution was a list of twelve "areas of inquiry" and "problems" that would characterize an ethnomusicology true to its double nature as both a form of anthropology and a form of musicology, both in pursuit of knowledge about humans as makers of music.

The twelve areas of inquiry were

1. shared cultural concepts about music;
2. the relationship between aural and other modes of perception (synesthesia);
3. physical and verbal behavior in relation to music;
4. musicians as a social group;
5. the teaching and learning of music;
6. the process of composition;
7. the study of song texts;
8. the uses and functions of music;
9. music as symbolic behavior (the meaning of music);
10. aesthetics and the interrelationship of the arts;
11. music and culture history;
12. music and cultural dynamics.

Merriam carefully reviewed the literature to provide overviews of each of these topics. He hoped to stimulate ethnomusicologists to adopt new approaches to research on music, and indeed he did.

"Mature" ethnomusicology

In the wake of Merriam's *The Anthropology of Music* and influential writings by John Blacking, the African ethnomusicologist J. H. Kwabena Nketia (b. 1921), and others, scholars in the new field of ethnomusicology slowly but surely began to create a rapprochement between the poles inherent in the discipline's name by writing more sophisticated and detailed studies of particular music cultures' musical sounds, conceptions, and behaviors. In 1980, at the twenty-fifth annual meeting of the Society for Ethnomusicology at Merriam's home institution, Indiana University, the organizers were confident enough to proclaim ethnomusicology's "coming of age." This newly mature ethnomusicology understood musical performance as fundamentally social. It had succeeded in erasing the distinction in early ethnomusicology between musicological and anthropological approaches to the study of music. Since then, the social-scientific and philosophical underpinnings of ethnomusicology have been strengthened, and the move away from the study of the "music sound itself" as an autonomous aesthetic domain has been decisive. As Christopher Waterman put it, "The irreducible object of ethnomusicological interest is not *the music itself*, a somewhat animistic notion, but the historically situated human subjects who perceive, learn, interpret, evaluate, produce, and respond to music." Even though lengthy analyses and characterizations of musical style, with associated transcriptions, have decreased, careful attention to musical detail still characterizes the best ethnomusicological research because, after all, the social is expressed in musical forms, structures, and performances.

If early ethnomusicology championed the study of supposedly older, "authentic" forms of traditional, world music uncontaminated by modern life, mature ethnomusicology, since 1978 or so, has moved enthusiastically toward the study of urban, popular, and hybrid forms of music. Today rap and reggae, *norteño* and Serbian *turbofolk*, Puerto Rican salsa and Jamaican dub, jazz improvisation and country music, the Eurovision song contest and piped-in music at the Mall of America, and new popular-music fusions in the world-music marketing category are as central to ethnomusicological inquiry as Japanese *gagaku*, Bulgarian folk music, Javanese gamelan, Hindustani classical music, and Native American drumming, dancing, and singing. By embracing modern musical practices, ethnomusicologists are better able to provide convincing answers to the question of why and how humans are musical.

Although ethnomusicology got its start when scholars from past and present imperial powers began to study music in all its variety the world over, another group of researchers entered the field intent on studying their own music as one step on the path to better self-understanding. Some of the earliest moves in this direction flowed from the civil rights and feminist movements of the 1960s and the resulting identity politics that sought a place at the scholarly table for minorities and women. In the United States, African Americans, Chicana/os, women, and Asian Americans began to ask new questions about their own music and its history and meaning from the perspectives of critical theory and cultural studies. Why, for example, is our music, the music of women, say, left out of the standard histories of music or the ethnographies of particular music cultures? Can we find the African roots of African American music in genres as diverse as the blues, gospel, soul, jazz, and rap? These scholars launched critiques of the ethnomusicological study of the Other, especially the way they contribute to structures of power and hegemony in the academy. They demanded that new methods and perspectives from inside their own cultures become part of the conversation.

In another development, ethnomusicologists' interest in all music and "music as culture" began to affect the work of scholars around the world who pursue studies of their own music. Many local traditions of musical scholarship focused principally on an analysis of musical sound structures and still do. Today, in addition to these once dominant musicological paradigms for the study of local traditional music, scholars in many parts of the world, some of them trained in American, British, and Australian universities, are turning to questions about the meaning and function of music in their own societies, to the notion of "music cultures." They are embracing multiculturalism, respect for other cultures, and the study of the music of ethnic minorities. In some locales these two approaches now exist in some tension, but elsewhere local and international forms of ethnomusicology are coming together to create fascinating dialogues on the question of why and how human beings are musical.

Since 1980, the comparative impulse of early ethnomusicology has receded into the background. Ethnomusicologists' desire to study human musical behavior in all its forms has tended to take the form of idiographic studies of particular musical cultures, genres, and scenes. To answer the big questions about why and how humans are musical, ethnomusicologists have spent the bulk of the last thirty years in an effort to champion, reveal, show respect for, understand, and document music in all its particular forms around the world.

Since about 2000, however, an interest in comparison may be reasserting itself. The evidence for this can be seen in books with titles such as *Deep Listeners: Music, Emotion, and Trancing*, *Music as Social Life*, and *Music and Technoculture*. Overview works like these, usually on particular themes, invite comparisons rooted in social or scientific theory rather than in comparative methods. In fact, comparative or generalizing studies are necessary if ethnomusicologists are to keep in balance their fascination with the way music works in particular cultures and their goal of contributing to a general understanding of human musicality.

Today, interest in world music and in the discipline of ethnomusicology is as high as it has ever been. The field has achieved a solid and respected, if still somewhat marginal, place in English-speaking universities, and growing recognition in universities around the world. At the same time it continues to question critically its purpose and potential to contribute to knowledge about, and the betterment of, humankind, and to open itself to new ways of studying and thinking about music.

Chapter 3
Conducting research

To further their goal of understanding why and how humans are musical, ethnomusicologists, like other scholars, study in libraries, archives, and laboratories. What makes ethnomusicological research unique among music disciplines, indeed one of its defining features, is that ethnomusicologists study in a place they call, metaphorically, "the field," a fertile ground where they toil for extended periods of a year or more in order to understand the nature of music in a particular place. During this fieldwork ethnomusicologists typically live in a community; participate in and observe and record musical events; interview musicians, their patrons, and audiences; and learn to sing, play, and dance.

Fieldwork sites

Although ethnomusicologists may focus, in a particular study, on a single musical performance, piece, repertory, genre, instrument, event, or performer, they almost always situate these items within the life of a society or group of individuals. Ethnomusicological research privileges the study of music as a social expression, that is, as a performance that emerges from, and is conducted by, individuals acting in groups united by social relationships and shared cultural knowledge. Those relationships and that knowledge may depend on a common language and heritage, territory, government, economic system, or other institutions, or they may depend on voluntary associations based on shared activities, interests, affinities, values, and beliefs.

In the early years of ethnomusicology, most studies were conducted within societies assumed to be tied together by geography. Geographical thinking has yielded studies of national music (Mexican music, Thai music) and of regions, cities, towns, and villages (music of Rajasthan, music in Shanghai). Societies can also be linked by cultural ties due to ethnicity, whether within a nation (Apache music in the United States, Ewe music of Ghana) or transnationally (Arab music); race (Black music); religion (Jewish music); or kinship (hereditary professional musicians of India). For the last twenty years or so, ethnomusicologists have been working in two other types of societies: communities based on affinity for a genre of music (heavy metal musicians and their fans), and communities defined by their association with institutions, for example, people making music in prisons, music conservatories, or bars and clubs.

These ways of thinking about the relationship between music and social groupings are not mutually exclusive. Very often societies and their associated musical practices are embedded within one another. Starting with an interest in African-derived music the world over might lead to a study of Black music in a national setting such as Brazil. Within Brazil, communities in the city of Rio de Janeiro and the state of Bahia have developed different musical practices. Social institutions like the Rio samba schools and Carnival support musical expression and make an interesting object of study. And samba as a genre has generated a community of fans in many parts of the world who gather locally and internationally to share their love of this musical form.

Choosing a fieldwork site and gathering data

How communities are selected for study has never occupied much methodological space in ethnomusicologists' accounts of their work. In the early years of the field's history, many ethnomusicologists selected the communities they studied based on a serendipitous encounter they had had with a particular musical style or community before they discovered the field of ethnomusicology. Perhaps they heard the music while serving abroad in the military or as the child of missionaries or after hearing it on a recording. In my own case, I became fascinated with Bulgarian and other forms of Balkan music when I joined an international folk-dancing group while in college. I discovered ethnomusicology a few years later and decided immediately to turn my love of Balkan music into an academic career.

In the late 1960s, when I came across ethnomusicology, it was taught principally as a graduate course of study in only a few universities in the United States. When ethnomusicology became established as a field of study taught at the undergraduate level in many colleges and universities, the pattern changed, and many students discovered ethnomusicology as a field that asked interesting questions about music before they imprinted on a music to study. This allowed students to choose a community to study based less on a fascination with the sounds of its music and more on the basis of a match between a musical culture and a question about musical cultures that they were interested in asking and answering.

Whatever accidents of personal history or rationalization guide ethnomusicologists' selection of a musical tradition and a fieldwork site, they eventually enter the field, establish rapport with musicians and community members, and obtain the so-called informed consent of those they will work with closely over the course of many months and years. In the early days, ethnomusicologists seem to have operated with two assumptions in mind: first, that the gathering of information about another culture's music (or even their own) was an ethically unproblematic search for objective knowledge about humankind; second, that they were neutral, machinelike collectors of data. Both assumptions have long since fallen by the wayside.

Ethnomusicologists now understand themselves to be historically and socially situated researchers engaged in conversations with historically and socially positioned interlocutors.

Understanding that the results of their research depend on conversations they have with people in the field, ethnomusicologists have reflected on the implications of the identities they bring into the field on the research process. Leading the way in this regard have been female researchers, who, although they may wish to be treated in a gender-neutral way, frequently find that the people with whom they work thrust a gendered identity upon them. The Finnish ethnomusicologist Pirkko Moisala, for example, describes how, working as a young woman with the Gurung of Nepal, her focus on male musicians and her attendance at all-male meals led the Gurung to regard her, in terms of kinship, as a "young son." As a consequence, she was not allowed to work with women and observe their musical world. Later, when she returned to the field with her own son, the women accepted her as an "older sister" and allowed her to listen to their music and stories, as she told them hers.

One of the most vivid stories of the problematic nature of data gathering comes from Paul Berliner, who worked in Zimbabwe (then Rhodesia) in the early 1970s with Shona musicians who played the *mbira dzavadzimu*, an instrument with twenty-three plucked metal keys attached to a flat piece of wood and placed inside a gourd resonator. Berliner discovered in a conversation with Mubayiwa Bandambira, an elderly expert on the instrument, that his curiosity about the music and the instrument was, from a local perspective, not a neutral and unproblematic search for knowledge. On numerous occasions Berliner asked Bandambira about the system for naming the keys of the *mbira*, and was given conflicting and incomplete information each time. After several visits, Bandambira, convinced of Berliner's sincerity, finally told him the proper names for all the *mbira* keys. Only then did Berliner realize that he had purposefully been given the runaround to test his seriousness and to teach him an important lesson about the privileged nature of cultural knowledge: it is not simply there for the taking by foreign ethnomusicologists intent on adding to the store of knowledge of humankind's music making. Not only do we choose our research subjects; they choose to work with us as well, sometimes, indeed usually, because they think they and their musical tradition will benefit from the interaction as well.

Although many individuals and communities may not have given much thought to protecting themselves and their traditions from inquisitive ethnomusicologists, some societies have. Aboriginal, native, and first-nation communities in Australia, the United States, and Canada typically require music researchers to seek permission not simply from the musicians themselves but also from community councils, and to deposit their research materials and reports with the community under study. The care that must be taken before embarking on fieldwork is not restricted to such cases, and today ethnomusicologists in the United States must submit a detailed research protocol for approval to their university's Institutional Review Board, which vets it to make sure that "human subjects" will be treated fairly and appropriately, and their privacy protected.

With the community selected, trust and rapport established, and with a plan for the ethical treatment of community members, fieldwork begins, typically with four main activities: interviews; participant-observation of musical events and community life; music and dance lessons; and audio and video recordings.

Interviewing

Ethnomusicologists interview people, sometimes formally and sometimes in casual conversations, to elicit oral histories, gather culturally specific insider musical knowledge about the musical tradition, and maintain rapport. The methodological necessity of acquiring insider knowledge surfaced in the 1970s in a productive confluence of ethnomusicologists' interest in how people conceptualize music and cognitive anthropology, which had developed methods for eliciting, in formal interviews, culturally meaningful categories and distinctions expressed in words. The notion of "meaningful distinction" was borrowed from linguistics, with its subdisciplines of phonetics, the study of observable differences in sound, and phonemics, the study of meaningful distinctions between sounds: for example, the phonetic difference between "r" and "l" is meaningful in English but not in some Asian languages. This difference in the study of language sounds led, in cognitive anthropology and ethnomusicology, to a distinction between "etic" analysis and "emic" analysis.

Using this framework, ethnomusicologists realized that one of their principal methods for understanding music, its transcription from sound into European musical notation and its analysis using the apparatus of European music theory (intervals and modes, meters and rhythms, timbres, textures, and forms) might yield an etic description of the music, perhaps useful for comparative purposes, but not to an emic, culturally informed understanding of how a musical tradition worked from the point of view of those making the music. Cognitive anthropology's mode of questioning gave them hope that they could find those meaningful musical distinctions in conversation with musicians.

Perhaps the most spectacular application of this method was the French ethnomusicologist Hugo Zemp's studies, published in the late 1970s, of instrumental classification and music theory among the 'Are'are people of the Solomon Islands. The 'Are'are subsist on domesticated pigs, fish, and root crops. They lack a system of writing but have an elaborate instrumentarium consisting of an astonishing array of panpipes made from bamboo. Zemp elicited their classification of these instruments by the way the instrument was played (struck or blown) and the way the pipes were tied together (in a row or in a bundle). He also uncovered the most elaborate system of descriptive musical terminology (in other words, music theory) that has ever been found among a people without a long tradition of literacy. The 'Are'are distinguish two sizes of intervals between adjacent pitches, which they call "big bamboo" and "little bamboo." Such a distinction is analogous to the one in European music theory between major and minor seconds. They also distinguish between different types of polyphony based on the number of parts (two, three, or four) and the relationships between the parts. Until Zemp's studies, ethnomusicologists had found such detailed music theory only in the literate cultures of Europe, Asia, and the Middle East, and they suspected that music theory and literacy were causally connected. 'Are'are music theory was a revelation. Emic analysis of this sort, gained from detailed interviews with musicians, has become a standard practice in the field.

Interviews are also used to elicit oral histories, including not just biographies but also kinship patterns among musicians and their musical experiences and values. One of the lengthiest examples is the "autobiography" of Frank Mitchell (1881–1967), a Navajo (or Diné, meaning "the people") ritual singer, elicited from interviews with the ethnomusicologists David McAllester and Charlotte Frisbie. Frank Mitchell was a specialist in a ritual known as the Blessingway, performed to maintain goodness within a person. By eliciting his life story, the ethnomusicologists, who placed themselves in the role of editors of the book rather than its authors, were able to study a number of themes of interest to ethnomusicologists including processes of enculturation; transmission of ceremonial material, including songs; interrelationships among myth, prayer, song, and ritual; Navajo cultural values and philosophy; the role and status of singers; cultural change; and the relationship between Frank Mitchell's role as a musical ritual practitioner and his other life roles, including husband, politician, tribal judge, and sawmill worker.

Focusing on life history is a way to elicit details about the relationship between music and culture in a manner that amplifies the voices of so-called native practitioners. Foregrounding oral history transforms the objects of ethnomusicologists' research into subjects, that is, the agents of their own histories. McAllester's and Frisbie's narrative—that assisted autobiography of Frank Mitchell—with its collaborative spirit and respect for the ethics of representation, was an early solution to the ethical problem endemic to the contexts in which ethnomusicologists conduct their research: the silencing, the world over, of the poor by the powerful.

Participant-observation

Talking to people is conducted in parallel with immersion in musical performance through participant-observation, a clunky anthropological term that captures the distance and the intimacy that characterize fieldwork. Ethnomusicologists, as a matter of method, hang out with musicians as they live their daily lives and as they travel to gigs, rehearse, and perform. What participant-observation as a method yields analytically are three kinds of event description: particular, normative, and interpretive. Ethnomusicologists begin, necessarily, with descriptions of particular events, but they hope to arrive at general or normative patterns of musical and social behavior that characterize all events of a particular type, say a wedding or a religious ritual or a concert. The ultimate goal is an interpretive description of the cultural meaning of a particular musical event. An interpretation may "read" the event as an instance of general values and processes at work in the culture and society, or it may show how the event does social or cultural work, for example by critiquing power relationships, illustrating newly imagined forms of social relations, or enacting new cultural values.

Analysis of musical events and their reading for cultural meaning was first called for in the 1970s as one way to create a bridge between musicological and anthropological modes of analysis. Such analysis is now a typical part of the narrative apparatus of ethnomusicological works. One of the most detailed and methodologically precise event narratives is Regula Qureshi's study of performances of Sufi Qawwali musicians in Pakistan. Qawwali are professional musicians who perform for gatherings of Sufis intent on going into trance as a way to become closer to God. The gathering, which can last all night, is socially stratified. Typically, only the poor lose themselves in trance while the wealthy, when moved by the music, resist trance but give money generously to the musicians. The lead singer, in performance, must single out those most likely to tip generously and those most likely to go into trance. He then walks a delicate musical path, at once pleasing the wealthy aesthetically and arousing in them a spiritual experience so they will give generous tips and, at the same time, sending those inclined to do so into trance. The lead musician molds each performance to serve his perception of the needs of those in attendance and his desire to make money. After interpreting some of the meanings specific to each event, Qureshi concludes by reading its meaning in terms of Sufi ideology and traditional social structures. Qawwali music, she argues, provides a way of expressing Sufi ideology, of giving form to the social life of a Sufi community, and of enabling various forms of individual expression. A detailed analysis of these kinds of musical events allows her to understand how these musicians and this community perform music, and why they do so in this particular way.

Learning to sing, play, and dance

Ethnomusicologists routinely learn to sing, to play musical instruments, and to dance in the traditions they study. What they learn depends on the culture's notion of what is appropriate for outsiders to learn and, often, on notions of gender. In some traditions, for example, only women sing or play certain kinds of drums. Some dances may be the domain of men and others of women.

The notion that such study should be a central element of fieldwork method was first articulated by Mantle Hood, a student of Jaap Kunst and an influential figure in the early history of the field. He called for ethnomusicologists to become "bi-musical" as a requisite for the serious scholarly study of music, first in the European musical tradition and then in a second one they were studying. The acquisition of bi-musicality is now a taken-for-granted part of the ethnomusicologist's tool kit, and is used wherever it can be appropriately applied.

What do ethnomusicologists learn when they learn to play the music of the people they are studying? First of all, they learn how music is structured and how it is brought to life in performance. Such detailed study often uncovers areas of musical practice that can be read for meaning. This happened to me during my work on Bulgarian traditional music, when, along with interviewing and participant-observation, I took lessons on the Bulgarian bagpipe, called *gaida*. While it was relatively easy for me to learn the physical aspects of playing the instrument and the basic structures of the music (its narrow-range melodic modes and its additive meters of 5, 7, 9, and 11), the dense ornamentation proved difficult to

2. Ethnomusicologist Anne Rasmussen (right) performs on the Arab lute, the *'ud*, with highly respected Indonesian Qur'anic reciter Ibu Maria Ulfah (left) and her colleagues at the Islamic boarding school Tebu Ireng in East Java, Indonesia. They are performing *tawashih*, songs in Arabic, with devotional poetry set to Arab melodies.

understand. Interviews were unhelpful. My principal teacher lacked a vocabulary to describe the ornamentation. He told me that I would have to wait until I acquired "bagpiper's fingers." Eventually, and independently of his instruction, I finally managed to acquire my own bagpiper's fingers. In the process I gained new understandings of the tradition, which I could express in words but that he could not. Even more fruitful, once I had acquired bagpiper's fingers, we could converse in finger motions: moving his hands in the air or on the instrument, he could now say to me in gestures, "do it this way"; "don't do it that way." Watching his fingers with the practice-based knowledge of my own bagpiper's fingers, I could interpret the meaning of the ornamentation. He told me, for example, that playing an ornament one way "filled his soul" because it referenced an old, rural lifestyle that he had grown up with. Playing it another way was emotionally "empty" because it referenced a modern manner of playing that had no meaning for him.

Documenting musical traditions

The fourth activity ethnomusicologists engage in during fieldwork is the documentation of musical performances and musical events in field notes and in audio and video recordings. Field notes, which are hardly specific to the field of ethnomusicology, have rarely been the object of much discussion. Apart from recording observations and experiences in the field, they also provide the opportunity to think through possible interpretations of what one has experienced earlier and to list new questions that flow from observation. They also act as a kind of therapy during what can be a trying ordeal intellectually, physically, and emotionally. Kay Kaufman Shelemay and Hiromi Lorraine Sakata are among the very few who have published personal, self-reflexive accounts of ethnomusicological fieldwork.

In the 1950s the invention of small portable tape recorders capable of making high-quality sound recordings transformed fieldwork. Before World War II, music researchers either relied on their ears alone, transcribing performances in the field into European musical notation, or they carried cumbersome recording devices like wax-cylinder recorders. Alan Lomax (1915–2002) and his father, John Lomax (1867–1948), both indefatigable recorders of American folk traditions, had to power their heavy recording devices in the trunk of their car with the aid of its battery. Being able to carry a tape recorder slung over a shoulder changed everything. Having permanent, replayable recordings enabled more accurate transcriptions and analyses of the structures of musical performances.

Faced with the problem of transcribing the dense polyphonic music of a Central African group who call themselves the Aka, the French-Israeli ethnomusicologist Simha Arom invented , in the 1970s, an elaborate recording technique. The musicians sing and play in many parts, but how the parts relate to one another is impossible to detect simply by listening to it. So Arom recorded each voice or instrument of a piece in sequence, using two stereo recorders synchronized together. After recording one part on one tape recorder, the second singer or instrumentalist listened to the recording on headphones and performed his part on a second, synchronized tape recorder. This continued until every musician had a chance to perform. The result was a recording of each part on a single channel plus a set of composite recordings built up in stages. With data gathered in this manner he was able to transcribe their polyphonic and polyrhythmic music, analyze it and finally deduce the underlying, normative models of vocal and instrumental performances, and how the particular performance of a piece was related to its model.

From the 1950s to the 1970s ethnomusicologists, faced with a dearth of recordings of the world's music traditions, took the highest quality recording equipment they could afford into the field with the goal, in some cases, of producing commercial high-fidelity LP records. Among the pioneers were Alan Lomax, who issued countless LPs of European and American traditional music; Paul Berliner, who produced two LPs of Shona *mbira* music; and

3. Ethnomusicologist Simha Arom plays back recordings he made on a previous field trip for Aka musicians and the community.

Philip Schuyler, who produced four LPs of Moroccan music. In the 1990s Philip Yampolsky produced an impressive twenty-CD survey of *Music of Indonesia* for the Smithsonian Folkways label. With the passage of time and the efflorescence of local recording industries and inexpensive cassette recorders, which even poor people could afford to buy to make recordings of their own traditions, the need for ethnomusicologists to make professional-quality recordings has declined. Many now use inexpensive, lightweight, digital recorders and small microphones, sometimes even recording in compressed rather than uncompressed formats.

Documenting musical performances visually was difficult and expensive until the release in 1983 of the first consumer camcorder using Betamax cassettes. Before that, ethnomusicologists mainly used expensive 16-mm film, and few had the skill or financial resources to do so. Exceptions included Hood, who made a documentary film about Ghanaian drumming called *Atumpan* in 1964; his student Robert Garfias, who documented a wide range of musical performances for national archives in the Philippines and

Korea in the 1960s; and Hugo Zemp, who has made films in the Solomon Islands, Switzerland, the Republic of Georgia, and Ivory Coast. Today, just as audio recording was once an indispensable tool, ethnomusicologists routinely carry lightweight video cameras into the field, and visual documentation has become almost de rigueur. Today, a few ethnomusicologists are using their field video footage to venture back into the realm, pioneered by Hood, of storytelling in documentary films.

Transcribing and analyzing music

Once back from the field, ethnomusicologists spend a lot of time analyzing the data they gathered there in a place they used to call, somewhat grandiosely, the "laboratory." When ethnomusicology was still emerging from its comparative, scientific phase, the lab might have included a sonograph for displaying sound waves, a tape recorder for playing back field recordings, often at half or quarter speed, and in a unique instance, a "melograph," a machine invented by Charles Seeger and his colleagues at UCLA to provide automatic transcriptions of individual melodic lines. Unfortunately, the detail the melograph provided was beyond the capacity of the researchers to interpret. They could find little or no meaning in the machine-produced graphs, and this innovation proved to be a dead end.

Although the scientific ethos of the field from the 1950s to the mid-1970s seemed to generate some enthusiasm for using machines to register musical sounds, and to help in their objective analysis, most of the effort to understand the structural elements of music was poured into laborious, handwritten descriptive transcriptions of the sound recordings that ethnomusicologists had made in the field. Substantial parts of doctoral dissertations, including my own, were filled with transcriptions of the repertoire under investigation. These volumes mirrored the practice of musical folklorists in Europe, who had been ostensibly preserving their folk traditions in this fashion for more than a century. The kind of detailed musical analysis such transcriptions make possible has, since then, largely passed out of vogue in Anglo-American ethnomusicology, though it is still an important component of some countries' ethnomusicological practice.

Today, transcriptions, rather than being collected in books and dissertations, are used to illustrate the author's narrative, which may include a characterization of the musical structures of a piece, performance, style, or genre and then go on to discuss how those musical structures express local psychological, cultural, social, economic, and political patterns and ideas. Some studies along this line could be accused of abandoning musical analysis in favor of interpretive readings of music's social and cultural significance, but most ethnomusicologists would agree that musical analysis is necessary to understand how a particular musical tradition works, what is distinctive about it, and how, precisely, it bears the personal, social, and cultural meanings attributed to it.

Intellectual property rights

In the first quarter-century of ethnomusicology, questions of the accuracy and reliability of transcriptions, as well as the development of reliable and valid methods for interviewing musicians and documenting musical performances, were extraordinarily important. In recent years those methods have become largely settled matters, and other issues have risen to prominence in relation to ethnomusicological fieldwork, perhaps none more important than the legal and cultural rights of those with whom we work.

When ethnomusicologists first made audio recordings in the field, they conceptualized the enterprise as scholarly and of no commercial value. In obtaining informal permission to make their recordings, they usually told the singers and musicians, quite honestly, that the recordings would be deposited and preserved in national, international, or university archives and libraries.

Furthermore, even had the ethnomusicologist wished to do so, there may have been no tradition of paying musicians for their performances. However, with the advent of world music as a commercial music category in the 1980s, and the easy exchange on the Internet of electronic sound files, this naïve reciprocity can no longer be sustained. Today, ethnomusicologists make and publish their recordings in a conflicted environment that requires the assertion of European and American notions of copyright and ownership, on the one hand, and an ethic of sampling that ignores such claims, on the other. Such ideas of copyright and ownership are, in turn, often not consonant with ideas and practices in the cultures being studied, catching the unwary ethnomusicologist in a complex web of competing and irreconcilable interests.

One of the most striking instances of this sort was reported by Hugo Zemp. His field recordings of music from the Solomon Islands were sampled in the 1990s by Deep Forest, a pair of techno musicians, for use in a song called "Sweet Lullaby" on their first album. The Deep Forest CD is a pastiche of techno beats and uncredited or miscredited traditional music that stereotypes "primitive" music and people in ways ethnomusicologists find abhorrent. Furthermore, they shared their profits neither with the Solomon Islanders nor with Zemp.

Even if well-intentioned ethnomusicologists, music samplers, and beat makers wanted to treat traditional recording artists fairly, the question of who owns music, once a strictly academic question, can be thorny. Whereas international copyright law exists to protect a singular creative work by a single author in a tangible form such as a recording or notation, in many cultures this notion of personal ownership is nonexistent: sometimes no one owns the music or everyone does. As Anthony Seeger has written about the Suyá Indians of Brazil, "How does one register a song composed by a jaguar, learned from a captive over 200 years ago, and controlled not by an individual but a ceremonial moiety?" According to American copyright laws, if a work has only ever existed in oral tradition, that is, in intangible form, then it is, by default, part of the public domain and can be used legally, if perhaps not ethically, by anyone without legal repercussions. In this kind of world, ethnomusicologists now must mediate among the groups they study, the recordings they make, and the globalized, commercial world in which some people are appropriating those recordings for their own profit.

Working in the field, getting to know musicians, their music, and their cultures, is probably ethnomusicologists' greatest joy. However, fieldwork as a method has been critiqued by some postcolonial and cultural-studies scholars as a potentially hostile act of "surveillance." But, as Titon has written:

> [T]hose who would condemn it shut themselves off from a valuable way of knowing that is constitutive of those disciplines (ethnomusicology, cultural anthropology, folklore) that employ it. As a way of knowing and doing, fieldwork at its best is based on a model of friendship between people rather than on a model involving antagonism, surveillance, the observation of physical objects, or the contemplation of abstract ideas.

Successful fieldwork is impossible without the friendship and cooperation of those with whom ethnomusicologists study. At its best, field "work" can feel more like play. But it must eventually be turned into interpretive and practical work: writing books and articles that answer questions about the nature of music, teaching in university settings, and helping people and communities with the everyday problems they face.

Chapter 4
The nature of music

Ethnomusicologists have made important contributions to understanding the nature of music from the vantage point of their fieldwork-based idiographic musical ethnographies. Arguably ethnomusicology's most important theoretical move has been a sustained attack over more than a half-century on the notion, purveyed until recently by its sister musicological disciplines, that music is primarily an art form made for its own sake, mystically transcendent in its effects, and with little or no social or practical significance. Combining the specificity of fieldwork with theories from anthropology and other social sciences, from feminism and other social movements, and from various philosophical traditions, ethnomusicologists have learned much about the nature of music as a human behavior and cultural practice in thousands of particular studies. In the process, they have created a rich picture of the nature of music and its significance for human life.

Ethnomusicological theories about the nature of music consist, implicitly or explicitly, of truth claims in the form of metaphors that link music to other domains of human thought. Among the most common metaphors are that

- music is a resource with psychological and social functions;
- music is a cultural form;
- music is a social behavior;

- music is a text to be read and interpreted;
- music a system of signs;
- music is art.

These metaphors, and others, can all coexist simultaneously or in sequence in any particular instance. They are based on theories being discussed broadly in the social sciences, humanities, and philosophy, and, taken together, they illustrate the richness of music's significance in human life.

Music as a resource

Probably the earliest form of ethnomusicological theorizing about the nature of music takes the form of claims about how music functions in culture and society and for individual human psychology. Traditional societies use music in innumerable ways across nearly all domains of life. Musical performances accompany nearly every important activity of cultural and social life, from birth to death and from work to rituals, religious ceremonies, leisure, and play. Beyond music's use in everyday life, ethnomusicologists working in the anthropological tradition known as structural functionalism asked how all these uses of music function in society, or, in more modern terms, how individuals and societies use music as a resource in aid of various psychological and social goals. While structural functionalism no longer guides the thinking of ethnomusicologists, the notion that music does something for human psychology and social life; that it has psychological and social functions; and that it is a resource that people call on for different purposes, is still firmly embedded in ethnomusicologists' thinking about the nature of music and its significance for human life.

Music as a social resource

Many cultures use music as a resource to integrate society around common, shared behaviors and values. In this strain of research, ethnomusicologists tend to claim that musical aesthetics and behavioral and cultural ethics are two sides of the same coin. When people are taught, for example, to make what the culture deems good music, they are also enculturated and socialized into ways of being good people and acting appropriately within that society. Sometimes this is done in song texts. For example, an African initiation ceremony may include songs that instruct young adolescents in proper adult behavior. Richard Waterman (1914–71) wrote of the Yirkalla Aborigines in Australia that

> throughout his life, the Aboriginal is surrounded by musical events that instruct him about his natural environment and its utilization by man, that teach him his world-view and shape his system of values, and that reinforce his understanding of Aboriginal concepts of status and of his own role.

Sometimes the enculturation occurs in the structures of musical performance. So, for example, if success in hunting depends on coordinated collaboration among the hunters, as it does among the forest-dwelling Aka people of central Africa, then their cooperative, interlocking, polyphonic singing before, during, and after hunting may prepare them for, and aid them with, that kind of work. School and patriotic songs help individuals feel connected to a social group and make them want to support that group and its values in competition or battle. Group performances, whether of large choral groups, massed bands, or synchronized dancers, enact social solidarity, provide a means for a community to see itself acting in social harmony, and experience itself in sync in an emotionally satisfying, intense, pleasing manner.

Music can also challenge powerful social institutions from positions of structural weakness. It can help to form communities where none have existed before, and to activate change in the underlying cultural assumptions and social structures of a society. For example, during the later years of the communist period in Bulgaria, the extravagant improvisatory virtuosity of Romani musicians playing modern instruments contrasted with the staid arrangements played by government-sponsored folklore ensembles playing traditional instruments. Those differences in musical style became rallying points for those who opposed the totalitarian government and its draconian policies with respect to Muslim minorities.

Music is also a communicative resource in music-filled events that humans have invented to celebrate the progression of life stages and the cycle of seasons. In these cases music fosters communication between members of a society. Among the Suyá Indians of the Amazon basin, for example, each ceremonial musical performance tells the Suyá something about the person who is performing and about the season in which it is performed. The Suyá year is divided into rainy and dry seasons. These seasons are established not by changes in the weather but by changes in the ceremonies performed and the songs that are sung. It is not simply the coming of rain but the singing of rainy season songs that communicates to one and all that the rainy season has begun. Singing also communicates a person's self-concept of his or her age category: child, adolescent, adult, or old person. A young boy might sing an adult song to signal his evolving sense of self. An aging adult male might begin to sing less forcefully to signal his passage into old age. An older woman, on the other hand, "might retain the sober demeanor characteristic of a younger woman." Anthony Seeger concluded that "every ceremony was the opportunity to reaffirm not only what one was (a male and a member of certain groups) but what one believed one was or wanted to be."

In another mode of communication, humans seem to believe nearly everywhere that singing, over and above ordinary speech, is necessary to communicate with gods, ancestors, and spirits. Often each moment of ceremonial liturgies and rituals is accompanied by a specific song or instrumental performance, implying that music has special powers to make the ceremony effective. Music is often the means used to contact the supernatural world and a sign in the natural world that such contact has occurred. African and African-derived spirit-possession ceremonies provide some of the clearest examples. In the religious traditions of *vodoun* in Haiti, *candomblé* in Brazil, and *santería* in Cuba, a pantheon of spirits is called on to possess devotees through dances, costumes, percussion rhythms, and songs particular to each one. In all these traditions a master drummer leads a percussion ensemble playing interlocking, polyrhythmic patterns. When the master drummer senses that a trained devotee is about to go into trance, he plays a particular pattern that helps the spirit enter the mind and body of the possessed.

When a social group cannot be heard, for example when it is suppressed by a more powerful group, music often provides members of that group with a noisy, heartfelt way to communicate their feelings, beliefs, and their very existence to another group. And the opposite is just as true. The powerful can use music to control space and push minorities and the powerless literally and figuratively into the periphery.

Music is routinely a resource for the identification of social groups, whether the moieties of an Amazonian society, royal lineages in stratified societies, political parties in modern societies, or social categories such as youth and adults, men and women, rich and poor. In these cases music functions as a symbolic identifier of the social group both to its own members and to outsiders. In popular music traditions such as punk or death metal, for example, musicians and fans maintain a strict adherence to a particular aesthetic—both sartorial and musical—that serves to identify them to each other and to delineate who is and who is not a member of the subculture.

Music as a psychological resource

Merriam listed three ways music might be said to function as a psychological resource: entertainment; aesthetic enjoyment; and emotional expression. Music clearly is an important resource in all manner of entertainments, from storytelling and dance to theater, film, television, and electronic games. In some cases, as in dance, it makes the entertainment possible; in others, it enhances the story with the emotional quality so often associated with music. Film music provides many examples of stereotypical musical gestures used to underline, and even create, romantic sentiment, fear, anticipation, and laughter.

Apart from its link to other forms of entertainment, people in most cultures use musical performance as a pastime, a distraction from the burdens of work and everyday life, and a lubricant for social interaction. In modern societies, professional musicians provide most of the musical entertainment, sometimes in concerts but most ubiquitously in recordings listened to on the radio, TV, CDs, and MP3 files through loudspeakers or on headphones.

Aesthetic enjoyment, which could be understood as a form of entertainment, seems to occur when people set aside musical performance, through special framing like a concert or a recording, as an object of contemplation. Rather than an entertaining diversion from either boredom or work or environmental noise, at concerts of music all other forms of stimulation are purposefully excluded so that intense focus can be placed on the musical experience.

Nearly everywhere musical performance seems to be an important resource for controlled emotional expression and the evocation of sentiment. The controlled nature of musical emotional expression contrasts to spontaneous outbursts of rage, sadness, or joy. For example, a Bulgarian woman I interviewed recalled an incident when, as a young bride, she felt slighted by her mother-in-law, with whom she lived along with her husband. When she burst into tears, she was counseled, "Stop crying; sing a song." She was being admonished, in other words, to channel her uncontrolled, shameful crying into the controlled, acceptable frame of singing. Singing can express not only the individual emotions of the performer but collectively felt emotions as well. Often a cathartic function has been attributed to singing, a way to let off steam and release tension, whether over a personal problem or the social rage of the powerless or the expression of feelings deemed inappropriate or even forbidden in everyday verbal interactions.

Music as a resource linking the psychological and the social

Music is used as a resource linking the individual and the social in two ways: physical response and agency. Because music is rhythmical, that is, it exists in time and often has a steady beat or pulse, it invites a physical response in those who hear it: snapping fingers, tapping feet, nodding heads, walking, marching, or dancing to the beat of the music. These shared responses provide a way for group members to bond together, understand and experience themselves as a social unit, and in some cases accomplish some special task, such as going to war as a unified and effective fighting force or working together efficiently. Acting together in rhythm to the music, people turn an individual psychological response into a social resource that brings communities, affinity groups, and entire societies into sync with one another.

Ethnomusicologists today also understand that individuals are agents who enact and challenge social norms, and use music as a resource to do so. Influenced by the work of the French sociologist Pierre Bourdieu (1930–2002) on practice theory, they have come to understand music as a nonverbal practice that can, outside verbal discourse, create gendered individuals and other socially constructed identities and subjectivities. For example, Christopher Waterman's study of a Yoruba *jùjú* musician and band leader in Ibadan, Nigeria, showed how that musician negotiated his relationship to two social groups: the upper classes for whom his band plays music; and the lower-class "band boys" whom he simultaneously cultivates and exploits. As a semiliterate musician, he works in the low-status, beggarly occupation of musician, along with other low-status musicians whose loyalty he must ensure in order to keep his band together. However, because people with money and wealth demonstrate their prestige through the hiring of the best possible musicians, he, as a very successful band leader, has been able to elevate his status to that of a person with some of the same money, prestige, and honor as his wealthy clients. The band leader's musical practice allows him to construct a self-identity that at once places him close to the social group of wealthy clients he plays for and at the same time keeps him not so socially distant from his band boys that they give up and leave his group to seek their fortunes elsewhere. He uses music as a resource to author himself.

Given even this short list of the ways humans use musical performance as a resource for achieving certain ends, ethnomusicologists are sometimes tempted to claim that music is as important as speech and language for individual humans and for human society. Not infrequently those we study support us in this view. As a Pueblo Indian from New Mexico once told the anthropologist Leslie White (1900–1975), "My friend, without songs you cannot do anything."

Music as a cultural form, music as social behavior

Two other metaphoric claims about the nature of music hold that it is a cultural form or social behavior that may be iconic of, or coherent with, other cultural forms and behaviors, a view derived from a form of structuralism propounded by the French anthropologist Claude Lévi-Strauss (1908–2009). One of the early studies along these lines, by Judith and Alton Becker, concerned the organization of time in Javanese gamelan music. Javanese gamelans, the largest orchestras outside the West, consist of a set of tuned bronze instruments, covering many octaves from enormous low-pitched hanging gongs to high-pitched, slab-key metallophones. Gamelan musicians create complicated polyphonic textures. Mid-range metallophones play the melody in even beats. Higher-pitched metallophones and tuned gongs subdivide the beats of the melody in half or in quarters to provide an elaboration of the melody. Low-pitched gongs provide an accompaniment that in some ways can be understood as simplifying the melody. The result is the simultaneous sounding of many rhythmic cycles going at different speeds. According to the Beckers, the multiple time cycles of Javanese gamelan music are coherent with, or iconic of, the Javanese concept of time, which is multiply cyclical as well: it is based on a system of weeks of different number of days. The coherence of musical and cultural forms creates a sense that these forms are "natural," even as they are culturally constructed.

In the 1960s Alan Lomax tried to work out the metaphor of music as social behavior in a vast comparative project labeled

4. Ethnomusicologist Mantle Hood illustrates the playing of the Javanese *rebab* (bowed lute). The knobbed gongs of a gamelan orchestra are visible in the background.

"cantometrics," a term he coined to capture his notion that song was a "measure of culture." He attempted to demonstrate on a global basis that the structures of song performance could be related to the performance of more general social relationships. He claimed that "within any one culture or subculture, singing is a rather standardized form of behavior," and that these musical standards are congruent with the culture's social organization: "A culture's favored song style reflects and reinforces the kind of behavior essential to its main subsistence effort and to its central and controlling social institutions."

Lomax's method involved collecting samples, submitted by anthropologists and others, of ten song performances from four hundred cultures from around the world. He then trained a team of "raters" to describe each example along thirty-six musical-style gradients, including melodic shape, loudness, "voice qualities, ornamentation, level of coordination, the rhythmic and musical organization of chorus and orchestra, the patterns of social organization in performance and how text is handled." Using statistical analysis, he made many claims about the relationship between song structure and social structure on a cross-cultural basis. One example:

> narrow intervals seem to be most frequent when there is much social stratification. The explanation may be that in a situation where one is continually addressing a person of higher or lower status restraints are imposed on the interaction so that it proceeds carefully—in small steps.

Lomax claimed that "for the first time, predictable and universal relationships have been established between the expressive and communication processes, on the one hand, and social structure and culture pattern, on the other."

Because ethnomusicologists, by the time of that study in the late 1960s, were moving toward intensive studies of particular cultures rather than extensive, comparative studies of this sort, their reaction to Lomax's attempt to create a universal theory for understanding music and its relation to society was quite negative. They complained about the methodology, gave examples of how, within the cultures they knew well, there were enough differences in musical style to resist Lomax's generalizations about a single dominant style and enough exceptions to his findings to make his statistical methods less than convincing.

While ethnomusicologists today might disagree with Lomax that relationships between song style and social style are predictable, they do tend to believe that music is a social behavior and that structural homologies between it and other social behaviors can be demonstrated through careful ethnographic work. The performance structure of North Indian classical music, for example, has aspects that seem to be homologous with, and explained by, the hierarchical social system of Indian society more broadly (conventionally known as the caste system). In the musical tradition, some vocalists known as Kalawants come from a higher social group than the accompanists (*sarangi*, harmonium, and *tabla* players). That social distinction parallels a musical structure in which melodic improvisation dominates. The accompanying *sarangi* or harmonium merely echoes the singer while the accompanying *tabla* holds the rhythmic cycle. The soloist contracts the concert, controls the structure of the performance, displays his artistry, and allocates how much money the accompanists make.

Among the Aymara Indians of the Peruvian Andes, musicians create new compositions collectively, a practice that is coherent with the collective ethos of the culture. In this instance, political leadership and musical leadership must always be exercised in relatively egalitarian group settings that involve everyone and that eschew direct argumentation. In music, while one man is an acknowledged "guide" and expert in music, a core group of music enthusiasts (*maestros*) collectively compose pieces for the

5. North Indian vocalist Ustad Yunus Husain Khan is accompanied by his relatives, who are also his disciples, on the two *tanpuras* at the rear, along with musicians from outside his family, Sita Ram on the *tabla* and Mahomood Dholpuri on the harmonium.

village panpipe ensemble. The process begins when someone creates a short melodic motif for a piece that will have an AA BB CC form. According to Turino:

> The initial brainstorming phase is often rather lengthy. If the men are not interested in certain material that is being offered, they will simply ignore it rather than directly rejecting it, just as they do with inappropriate ideas offered in decision-making meetings in [town]. After a period of time, if a musician gets no reaction to the phrase or motives he is playing, he will drop them and try something else or simply fall silent. When an idea is found promising, however, others will gradually take notice, stop what they are doing, and join in softly on their instruments until everyone has taken it up.

Musical composition in this case is clearly a form of social behavior carried out in a way consistent with political decision making. Based on this example, it is probably not too far-fetched to understand musical composition in European classical music as a social behavior coherent with ideas of individualism, talent, and heroic achievement in the culture at large.

Music as text

The 1980s and early 1990s were the heyday of this sort of structuralist analysis. While ethnomusicologists continue to view music as a form of social behavior and as a cultural form, their search for homologies and coherences among them has been short-circuited by a move to poststructuralism. Poststructuralism rejects static homologies between music and cultural or social structures in favor of the study of the dynamic production, through musical performance, of social and cultural meanings. It is a move, in other words, away from the notion that music "reflects" culture to the idea that music can be productive of culture. Influenced by Clifford Geertz's (1926–2006) interpretive anthropology, ethnomusicologists in this mode interpret or "read" the meaning of music and musical performance regarded as texts. The object of interpretation is to lay out in as much detail as possible the cultural motivations, meanings, and systems implicit in, and thus explaining, specific actions.

One of the earliest and clearest examples of the use of this metaphor of music-as-text was a study of musical life in an American conservatory of music. The author, Henry Kingsbury, interpreted students' solo recitals, a typical capstone degree requirement, as an enactment of American individualism, a ritualized performance that has the potential to validate students' professionalism or expose them as untalented or not yet ready for the status of professional musician. This emphasis on evaluation of the individual's talent and preparation for professional life is part of a "cultural system" in which a recognition of differences in talent and ability are so pervasive that they take on an almost sacred character; hence, the ritualized nature of the solo recital as an expression of those beliefs and values. Kingsbury claims that "a solo recital [is] a rite in a cult of the individual. . . . The continuing efficacy of the recital as a ritual in such a cult requires that some, but not all, succeed." Such rituals are necessary to give life to a cultural system that values individuality. "The cultural value of individualism is not . . . airborne, [but is] produced and reproduced through ritual action," and the solo musical recital is one of many such rituals in this cultural system. Such interpretations are dependent on a deep understanding of the cultural system being "read." Getting to the point of making such confident readings takes long-term immersion in the culture through fieldwork. It is also easy to see how such readings stand apart from how the actors themselves may read and intend their own actions.

Music as a system of signs

The ethnomusicological search for musical meaning has been at odds, until recently, with thinking in the fields of historical musicology and music theory. Scholars in those fields have been impressed by the differences between music and language. Whereas in language, English speakers agree about the meaning of a word like "tree," no such consensus about the musical meaning of, say, a minor scale seems to exist, leading them to conclude that music has no meaning, or at least no shared meaning worth discussing. Ethnomusicologists realize that, while they may never find the musical equivalent of "tree," they frequently observe human beings assigning meanings to musical features and performances just as they assign meaning to other cultural forms such as clothing, food, and physical gestures. Often these meanings arise from distinct historical and social positions, and so they differ from group to group or individual to individual or time to time.

The problem of these differing interpretations of musical meaning has been clarified by recourse to semiotics, the "science of signs," especially the version propounded by the American philosopher

C. S. Peirce and explicated in detail for music study by Thomas Turino. Semiotics distinguishes three types of signs: symbols, indexes, and icons. Each operates according to different logics. Language uses symbols, that is, signs with specific, predictable meanings. Musical analysis and musicological interpretation depend on linguistic symbols. Turino argues, though, that symbols take us away from the direct experience of music. They are not at the core of musical meaning, and they fail to explain why people find music so meaningful and moving. He points rather to indexes and icons as sign types that encode the experience of music in direct and unmediated ways.

An index is a sign that points to the object it represents. This occurs in music when a particular piece or practice is associated with or occurs at the same time as something else. An obvious example would be a national anthem with patriotic text performed on political occasions. Pretty soon the anthem becomes a widely shared index of patriotism, and it can generate feelings of patriotism whenever played, say, before a sporting match, and even when played instrumentally without its lyrics. Such instances point to the possibility of shared musical meaning through shared associations and personal experiences. Just as important for musical experience are indexes that are personal and individual, the classic example being the "our song" phenomenon, a song shared by two people in love; the song, as index, can generate strong feelings in the absence of the beloved and even long after the flame between them has cooled.

An icon is a sign that resembles in some way the thing it represents. The religious icon, a two-dimensional painting of a three-dimensional person, gives this type its name. Common musical icons include flutes imitating bird songs, ascending melodies representing joy or ascent into heaven and descending ones representing a descent into hell, and extravagant improvisation taken as an icon of personal freedom or the triumph of the individual over the system. Sometimes the interpretation of musical icons depends on the experience of the listener. At other times, as when people hear a piece as an icon of familiar music they have heard before, listeners can imagine themselves as part of the social group that makes that kind of music. Understanding a musical gesture as an icon is an act of imagination that contributes to a person's sense of identity and triggers the strong emotions associated with that identity.

Turino concludes that music "involves signs of direct feeling and experience," specifically icons and indexes. While music can be read for meaning just as language can be, it is, after all, a different kind of sign system from language. Music does something else for humankind besides creating meaning, something just as important. According to Turino:

> When people shift to symbolic thinking and discourse [as in language] to communicate about deep feelings and experiences, the feeling and reality of those experiences disappear and we are *not* satisfied. This is because we have moved to a more highly mediated, generalized mode of discourse, away from signs of direct feeling and experience. Symbols . . . fall short in the realm of feeling and experience. That is why we need music.

Another factor that makes music so potentially rich in meaning is the complexity of its nature as a sign. Music as a sign has many elements, and each can be an icon or index with meanings that reinforce or contradict one another. The elements of music include melody, meter and rhythm, the timbre or sound quality of instruments and voices, the weaving together of many melodies or rhythms into textures and harmonies, and performance choices like tempo, dynamics, and articulation. A modern Bulgarian postsocialist musical genre called "popfolk" uses different elements of music to construct a complex sign pointing to competing imagined identities. Synthesizers, drum sets, and electric guitars produce an underlying bed of amplified sound that is an icon of modern forms of global popular music. This element in the musical sign allows Bulgarian fans of this music to imagine themselves as modern and connected to a cosmopolitan culture in which this kind of music is ubiquitous. The lyrics are in Bulgarian, and sometimes a Bulgarian traditional instrument like the bagpipe is added to the mix, underscoring the Bulgarianness of this genre and its link to Bulgarian national identity. Some of the genre's best musicians and singers are Roma, and so the genre features brilliant instrumental solos on clarinet and saxophone in nonmetrical styles and rhythms iconic of Romani and Turkish musical styles and genres, helping to create a sense of identity that acknowledges and even celebrates Bulgaria's Ottoman past and Bulgarians' distance from a pan-European identity. The cross-cutting and conflicting musical icons in this genre lead Bulgarians with different senses of Bulgarian identity to respond emotionally to it in very different ways. The complexity of music as a sign partly explains why music is such a powerful bearer of musical meaning and emotion.

Music as art

Even though ethnomusicologists have spent most of their time developing alternative metaphors to the notion that music is an art, in the end, that metaphor is virtually inescapable. Claiming that music is an art, however, opens up a question that has proven remarkably elusive to answer, namely: What is art? To oversimplify, definitions of art exist at two extremes. At one end and for most of its history, European thought has held that art is the skillful making of something; it is synonymous with mastery of a skill or craft like painting, cabinet making, or playing music. Art as skillful execution leads to such locutions as the art of war or the art of medicine. This definition puts a great deal of emphasis on the makers of art. Although developments in European philosophy since the eighteenth century have largely supplanted this older definition, ethnomusicologists continue to embrace it because of its emphasis on the making of art and on human agency. This definition's avoidance of a distinction between fine art and functional art, that is, between art and craft, fits ethnomusicologists' worldviews rather well. Art by this definition exists in every culture on earth, and ethnomusicological studies of those cultures are filled with fascinating accounts of musical skill and craft, in other words, musical art.

The other extreme of European definitions of art is indebted to Immanuel Kant's (1724–1804) *Critique of Judgment* (1790). It emphasizes the experience of the listener and links art to aesthetic judgments of the beautiful, the sublime, the good, and the agreeable. In effect, after Kant art and aesthetics became almost synonymous. This view of art focuses on the ability of art, and the "artwork," to express emotions (as music often does); represent or imitate something beyond the work (as paintings and sculpture often do); possess formal elements worthy of interest and contemplation for their own sake ("the music sound itself"); and generate sensory experiences that can be judged aesthetically as beautiful or ugly, tasteful or gauche, and so forth. Such aesthetic verdicts are based on substantive qualities supposedly in the artwork itself, qualities such as elegance, balance, complexity, and the like.

As the previous discussion of metaphors should have made clear, ethnomusicologists find plenty of evidence in a wide variety of cultures of music as a resource to express emotions and as a text or sign system that represents something beyond music. The other two parts of the definition are more problematic for them, however.

The idea that music is an art with formal properties worthy of contemplation for their own sake might lead to research similar, in some respects, to the search for skill and craft in the first definition of art, and it comes naturally to European-trained ethnomusicologists. Like all musicians, ethnomusicologists have spent hours acquiring the craft of making music. When they hear others make music, they want to know how the music works, how the elements come together to make a coherent performance or a "work" of music. In ethnomusicology this curiosity about the products of musical thinking is satisfied through extensive musical analysis, sometimes using transcriptions or notations produced by the musical culture under study. This type of detailed formal analysis of works and performances of music as art declined after about 1980 in favor of research that used other metaphors to situate music within culture and society.

In the last decade, though, analysis of the formal properties of world music has been resurrected under the leadership of the composer and ethnomusicologist Michael Tenzer. He and his colleagues seek to "inscribe and analyze musical structure to journey attentively into it, to experience each performance/piece/sound-world as a singular, textured, and refined event." These goals reposition ethnomusicological study within a European, universalizing definition of what art is in contrast to the last thirty years of ethnomusicological work, which justified the formal analysis of music as a method to understand culturally specific instances of music as a skill or craft, a cultural resource, a social behavior, and the like. Careful attention to the formal properties of musical works can provide one type of answer to the question of how humans are musical in particular instances, and Tenzer holds out the hope that it may lead, as well, to the discovery of common principles governing human musicality and thus to an understanding of our common humanity.

This view of music as art, in the Kantian sense, creates many problems for ethnomusicologists. The first is that it has been used to valorize a limited, European view of art as always about beauty and to relegate non-European practices to a category of non-art or functional or applied art. Ethnomusicological research, using a combination of many metaphors about the nature of music, shows that even European musical art may have nonaesthetic social, cultural, and political functions, and that many cultures, though by no means all, make their own specific judgments about what is good and beautiful in music. In other words, the substance on which verdicts of beauty are made are culturally specific and not universal.

The second problem is that, as Turino suggests, music may not be "a unitary art form, but rather . . . [it] refers to fundamentally distinct types of activities that fulfill different needs and ways of being human." He distinguishes four types of musical art: participatory live performances, presentational live performances, high-fidelity recordings, and "studio audio art" recordings. He maintains that each type needs to be judged according to its own goals, not from a single, universal perspective about the nature of music.

Ethnographic cases in which aesthetic judgments of the formal properties of art or its effect on the emotions are missing constitute a third problem with this definition of art for ethnomusicologists. Writing about his research on Navajo (Diné) music, for example, David McAllester recounts how he thought he was asking a question about "esthetics and personal preference" when he asked them how they "felt" when they heard certain kinds of singing. He was surprised when they answered something like, "I'm all right. There is nothing the matter with me." Because so much of Diné music is used to cure physical and mental illnesses rather than for aesthetic enjoyment and contemplation, McAllester learned that questions about aesthetics offended his interlocutors, who thought he was implying that they were ill. A "good" performance in this case is one with enough intensity to heal the sick, not to create an aesthetically agreeable sensory experience.

A fourth problem for ethnomusicologists with this definition of art is their concern that the link between aesthetics and art is not autonomous. Rather, they are wont to observe that powerful institutions often confer on musical practices the status of "artworks" and define what art is. Ethnomusicologists routinely teach in one such institution, the university music school or college music department, many of which perpetuate a particularly narrow view of musical art devoted exclusively to so-called Western art music.

Understanding music metaphorically as a resource that functions psychologically and socially; as a cultural practice or social behavior homologous or coherent with other cultural and social practices; as a text that can be read for meaning; as a system of signs capable of provoking deep feelings and emotions and new social understandings; and as an art does not exhaust ethnomusicologists' contribution to the study of the nature of music. Their studies along these lines, however, do provide an important corrective to the notion that music is merely an art for its own sake. By making these metaphors, ethnomusicologists have amplified significantly the claims, made from ancient times to the present, that music is essential to the enterprise of being human and of acting humanely in the world.

Chapter 5
Music as culture

Societies are linked, in part, by a shared culture. Anthropologists, who developed the culture concept in ways very different from the term's earlier associations with "civilization" and "taste," have defined it in a dizzying variety of ways. Ethnomusicologists, who rely on the culture concept to a great extent, have not troubled themselves very much with its definition, but they typically claim that music is culture. Culture in this sense refers to all forms of human knowledge, creativity, and values, and to their expression in music, language, cosmology, religion, ethics, plastic arts, dance, the making and use of tools, dwellings, cooking, clothing, and body decorations. Ethnomusicologists believe that humans make music as a constituent element of culture, and much research has been devoted to demonstrating connections between music and other facets of culture.

Because cultures are so complex, ethnomusicologists study these connections between music and culture principally through studies of particular cultural themes, issues, and questions. Some of the oldest and most enduring themes, such as those listed in Merriam's *The Anthropology of Music*, have included the study of native concepts about music, which in traditional cultures are often linked to cosmology and religion; the teaching and learning of music; the social behavior of musicians; the coherence of music with the other arts; the meaning of music; and the relationship between musical and cultural change. Oddly, although a tremendous amount of the world's music accompanies dance and Merriam was interested in "physical behavior" with respect to music, the study of dance did not find a place in his list of themes. In fact, ethnomusicological publications and conferences have always welcomed reports on dance research, and it deserves a place among the important themes of the field.

From the mid-1960s to the early 1980s, new issues came to the fore, including studies of urban and popular music, and the challenge of modern life to traditional music; music's role in religious experience, including trance and other euphoric states; and patronage and the economics of music. From the early 1980s to 2000 ethnomusicologists turned their attention to gender and music; the effect of media and technology on music; music, politics, and power; individual agency in culture; social and individual identity; and the effect on music of migrations, diaspora, and globalization. In the first decade of the new millennium, yet more themes have been added to the list, including music in relation to war, violence, and conflict; music's potential to ameliorate pandemics such as HIV/AIDS; and the role of music in cultural memory and nostalgia. It is not possible in this very short introduction to deal with all these themes. Some of the newest ones will be treated in chapter 8, but here are five that illustrate how ethnomusicologists have used them to show that music is culture.

Local concepts about music

Each culture has a specific set of beliefs about the origins of music, its role and significance in society and culture, its proper performance, how it is classified and described, and how it is valued. For example, while in European culture we generally believe that music is an unmitigated good ("That's music to my ears"), in cultures influenced by a particularly strict interpretation of Islam, music is evil because of its association with wine and women, and because it distracts believers from their proper religious duties. The Taliban's banning of music in Afghanistan is only the most famous instance. On the other hand, devotees of a variant strain of Islam known as Sufism believe that musical performance, singing, and sacred dance are paths to union with God.

Ideas about the origin of music are endlessly fascinating in their cultural specificity. Sometimes such explanations reach deeply into the culture's cosmology, and sometimes they are rooted in social life. I recall asking Todora Varimezova, a Bulgarian singer with a large repertoire of songs, where her songs came from. A strain in folk-music research claims that the creation of folk song is communal, an expression of the people. This notion fits the nationalist ideology that motivates much folk song collecting. So I was delighted when Todora answered, "A sharp-witted woman made them up." The answer clarified an important point about Bulgarian songs and their singing and their position in village social life. They flowed only indirectly from a "folk culture"; they were, more directly, the expressions of, and responses to, the real-life experiences of women in Bulgarian culture.

Another strand in research on musical concepts elicits local classifications of musical genres and types and the language they use to describe the formal properties of music. The 'Are'are case (see chap. 3) was perhaps the most spectacular, but there are many others. The rain-forest-dwelling Kaluli of Papua New Guinea, for example, routinely hear the sounds of water flowing in rivers and over waterfalls. Steven Feld documents how they use their experience of those sounds as metaphors for a highly technical music-descriptive language that deals with composition, melodic intervals, rhythm, and vocal style. When they speak about melody, for example, they distinguish descending minor thirds from descending major seconds in the pentatonic scale. The minor third in a descending melodic passage is called "waterfall" and is "a symbol of sadness, isolation and loss." When songs descend to the tonal center, they are said to make a "waterfall sound," and when a melody sits for awhile on the tonal center, then it resembles "continual waterfall flow." When a melody rests on a pitch before descending, it is likened to the ledge before the water falls. The melodic descent to a level pitch is described by terms referring to the still pool at the bottom of a waterfall. The Kaluli possess not just labels for aspects of their musical practice but also a systematic music theory, which borrows from, and is coherent with, a way of thinking about their world more generally.

Music teaching and learning

John Blacking believed that music was a fundamental attribute of human nature, as important to us as speech and language. He based this claim on his study of the Venda people of South Africa, a supposedly egalitarian society. Among the Venda all people learned to be musical (to sing, to play panpipes, to dance, or to participate through hand-clapping and other gestures) just as they all learned language and all the tasks necessary for subsistence. From this Blacking concluded that economic stratification and specialization of labor in larger societies led to the creation of classes of specialist and professional musicians, and a corresponding de-musicalization of the majority of the population, a loss of capacity caused by capitalist economies, one that diminishes the quality of human existence.

The question, Blacking believed, of who gets to learn music and how widely or narrowly it is distributed in a particular culture is one with important moral implications. Beyond egalitarian societies like the Venda, music is available for everyone to learn where children's music is an important childhood activity; where it is a required part of initiation into adulthood; or where it is an obligatory feature of adult socializing. In Flathead Indian society in the United States, for example, Merriam found that all men must learn a powerful song during their adolescent "vision quest." After days of nutritional and sleep deprivation in the wilderness, a spirit, in the form of an animal singing a song, approaches the man. As the animal gets closer, the song becomes clearer to the vision-seeker, who learns it and uses it throughout his life for good luck in many circumstances. Every man must learn and be able to sing such a song to be successful in life, love, and gambling.

In societies where music is available for all to learn, especially all with enough money to pay for music lessons or who are born into the right social circumstances, the observed unequal distribution of skill, ability, and interest in music is often attributed to talent. Euro-American culture provides an archetypal example of this view. If talent is not invoked to explain the unequal distribution of musical skill in a society, it is often attributed to the availability of musical experiences in childhood or a kind of genetic inheritance: "it is in the blood." Often musical families provide ideal learning contexts for music, and thus they tend to perpetuate themselves and the traditions they embrace. In the United States famous musical families include the Seegers, the Guthries, the Carters, and the Jacksons; the Copper family in England; and the Bachs and Mozarts in Central Europe.

Learning music, especially new songs, is attributed, in some cases, to supernatural contact and dreams. In what seems to be a more widespread practice than among the Flathead, only certain individuals, called in some cases shamans, have the capacity to learn songs from supernatural sources. They become either the sole performers of such powerful music, or they teach others in society the songs they learn in dreams or ritualized moments of contact. Anthony Seeger told the story of a Suyá (Amazonian Indian) man named Takuti, who explained that witches pull a sick man's spirits from him and take it to the birds, where the spirit hears their songs. Although he may return to health and appear normal, he is said to be "a man without a spirit." He is viewed, like a composer, as a source of new songs that he heard while his spirit was among the birds. He then can teach these songs to others, when they request a new song.

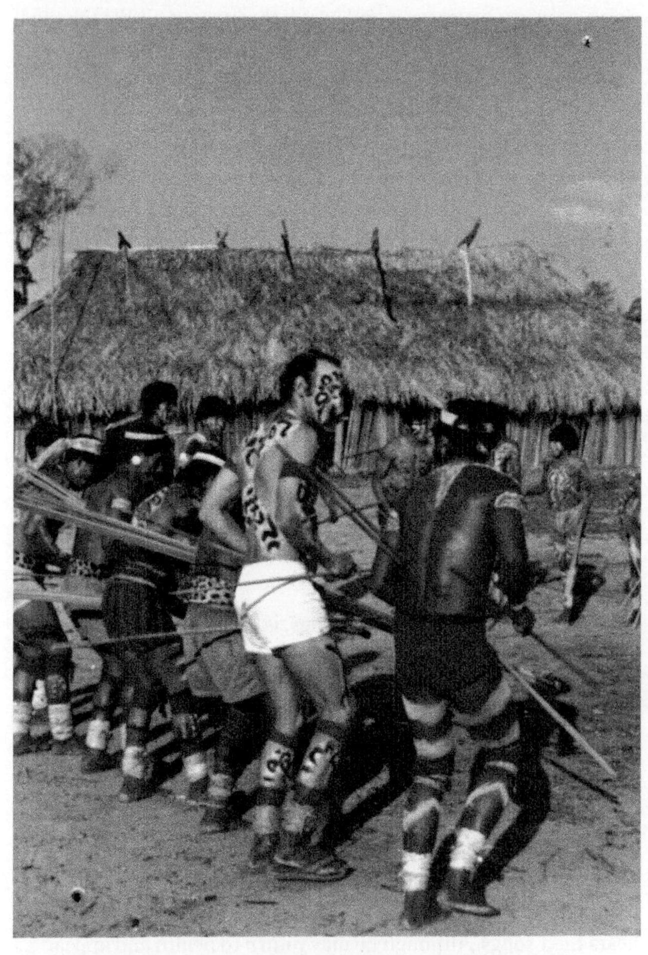

6. Anthony Seeger dances with the Suyá in the center of the village where he studied Suyá music and culture.

Even when music is available to all, access to certain parts of a culture's repertoire may be restricted by class, race, ethnicity, age, gender, or occupational background. Gender is perhaps the most-reported social factor limiting access to music learning. In many cultures men and women have separate repertoires or must learn different singing styles and different instruments. As traditional societies encounter modern life, aesthetic preferences and changing values are often cited as a means of overcoming restrictions based on social categories. In Bulgaria, where women traditionally did not play musical instruments, a woman I knew chose, over her parents' objections, to play the bagpipe (*gaida*) because she was attracted to its sound. Having crossed one culturally constructed boundary between appropriate behaviors for men and women, she went on to become the principal teacher of the instrument at the national conservatory devoted to folk music. In a case where many styles are available to choose from, Paul Berliner reported that jazz instrumentalists, who are overwhelmingly male, chose jazz over blues, gospel, soul, rap, classical, or other genres available to them using a number of factors, including "love at first sound," the technical challenges of jazz, the opportunity for improvisational creativity, family and peer approval, and its function as a "symbol of rebellion" and a "rejection of black middle-class values."

Identity and music

Since the early 1980s arguably the most ubiquitous theme in ethnomusicology concerns the way music contributes to the formation of individual and social identities. The interest in identity reflects a shift away from an understanding of traditional social life as consisting of a set of preexisting roles and structures into which individuals inevitably fall by virtue of accidents of birth: man/woman; rich/poor; rural/urban; ethnicity; or a hereditary occupation. Instead, modern life seems to grant to many individuals some agency in the construction and performance not of social roles but of "identities." An interest in identity represents a shift from structuralism to poststructuralism and from sociological, group-centered explanations to psychological, individual-centered ones. The focus on identity seems to reflect a departure from worlds that ethnomusicologists constructed as "traditional" to ones they construct as "modern." In the modern world individual agency is foregrounded to help explain the complexities of people on the move, whether because of social mobility and choice within their own societies, or emigration from a specific, traditional place into a globalized, transnational modern space where people need to construct new individual and social identities.

One strain of research along these lines asks what role music plays in the construction of identity. For example, according to Peter Manuel, the genre *salsa* has become an important symbol of identity for Puerto Ricans and Nuyoricans (Puerto Ricans living in New York City). Although *salsa* has its roots in Cuba, where musicians combined American big-band music and African-derived drumming, Puerto Ricans understand it as "theirs." To construct their own identity, they have bracketed its historical roots in Cuba and given it new meaning as a symbol of a sense of identity that is urban, cosmopolitan, and Latin American. The enormous popularity of *salsa*, aided by electronic media, extends well beyond a particular social class, ethnic subgroup, or age. It can speak to and for the entire group in a positive way that counters the discrimination they experience living in ethnic enclaves in New York.

Ethnomusicologists have also argued that musical performance helps to construct a social identity by providing a sonic sign of difference from, or a boundary between, other ethnic or social groups. According to Chris Goertzen, the small Occaneechi band of Native Americans in the state of North Carolina has tried to use music in this way. They, like other tribes of North Carolina, have lost their original musical traditions and have taken up the powwow tradition from the central Plains region of the United States. Native American groups in North Carolina began performing powwows in the 1960s as a way to assert difference from the White culture that was being forced on them. "Powwows are the main tool North Carolina Indians have for defining their collective identity to outsiders. . . . Indians use powwows to encourage the surrounding communities to respect both the nature and the boundaries of their communities." Unfortunately, the Occaneechi took up the powwow and its music much later than did the other tribes. The North Carolina Commission of Indian Affairs, made up of members of Indian tribes in the area and possessing the power to decide who is Indian and who is not, have so far denied the Occaneechi's application for Indian status and identity. They do not accept Occaneechi performance of powwow music as an unambiguous symbol of Native American identity. Further complicating the matter, most non-Indians do accept this particular symbolism. Musical practice in relation to identity works for the Occaneechi in one way (a sense of belonging and self-understanding), for other tribes not at all, and for Whites as a symbol of a specific, "different" kind of identity.

If communities use music to create boundaries between themselves, individuals sometimes use music to blur boundaries between social identities, whether it be a female rock guitarist smashing her instrument on stage to make a claim for a form of female identity beyond supposed norms, or suburban White youth drawn to African American urban hip-hop as a way to imagine an identity not defined by race or place.

In study after study, ethnomusicologists have shown how centrally important music can be to the construction, self-representation, and contestation of individual and social identities.

Gender and music

Early ethnomusicological studies tended to treat musical cultures as unified, as a set of ideas and practices shared by all within a particular society. Eventually feminist scholars noticed that women's musical performance and experience were often left out of the stories. Ellen Koskoff introduced this theme in a collection of essays, published in 1989, called *Women and Music in Cross-Culture Perspective*. In the wake of this intervention, ethnomusicologists routinely study how musical styles and performance register gender differences. Sometimes they find that male/female gender duality is linked to other dualities in a culture's ideology: public/private; expressive/modest; rational/emotional; and sacred/profane. In other cases, ethnomusicologists study how musical performances support or challenge power differences between men and women, and Koskoff's collection contains a number of telling examples. Some Moroccan Berber songs, for example, may criticize a prospective groom in an arranged marriage and thus save the girl from an unfortunate fate, but they do not challenge the existing social practice of arranged marriages. In Euro-American culture, on the other hand, all-female choirs have been formed to create a performative space where supposed female values of cooperation and independence from men can be safely worked out. The basic claim in cases like these is that musical performances dramatize the social order and, in the process, open up possibilities for change in that order. The possibility for social and cultural change through music flows logically from the belief that music is itself powerful, whether because it enables communication with the supernatural world, heals the sick, moves listeners to experience powerful emotions, or creates a groove that unites a group in emotional fellowship.

Another question concerning music and gender asks how music participates in the enculturation of gendered identities. Among Muslim Albanians living near Lake Prespa in Macedonia, men's and women's performances of a three-part polyphonic singing style reinforce and "engender" the gendered norms of behavior within a patriarchal system. Women sing in a chest voice in a high tessitura, a voice they call "thin," and in a quiet "relatively subdued" manner governed by a metrical beat. This way of singing is an icon of the controlled, modest female behavior demanded of them in this culture. Men sing nonmetrical songs with a wider range and a loud, tense voice. These performance features allow men a good deal more freedom of expression than the style given to women. As Jane Sugarman notes, when men and women sing in different ways, they "experience themselves in gendered terms." She also contends that the two different singing styles encourage those in this Albanian community to view each gender as

> innately very different, as opposites who need each other to exist. . . . As they participate in weddings, [they] are called upon to reinscribe not only their sense of a gendered self, but also that self as embedded within a particular form of patriarchal society. . . . Through their actions, the particular form that their society has taken, with all its gendered implications, emerges not as an arbitrary construct but as an essential and inevitable component of the natural order.

Singing, in other words, is a nonverbal practice that enacts a cultural system and set of values that seem natural to the members of this society.

Music, trance, possession, ecstasy, and emotion

One of the most dramatic experiences, literally, that an ethnomusicologist can have is watching people go into trance during a musical performance. Suddenly and without warning, adepts of a particular religion that sanctions trance may jump to their feet and begin dancing energetically in the recognized style of a god; or, after shrieking and gesticulating, they may pass out; or they may begin to talk and act, not like themselves but like an ancestor or an animal spirit. Only slightly less striking, male audience members at a concert of Arab secular music may be transformed from well-dressed, dignified listeners sitting passively at banquet tables into disheveled, excited, gesticulating, shouting, ecstatic enthusiasts standing next to the stage. And then there are those individuals who are moved to tears by a particular musical performance. Are these all variable reactions to a similar psychosocial phenomenon, the power of music, or are they distinct? Does music's ability to move people emotionally and even into ecstatic or trance states depend on its formal qualities, say fast, repetitive beats, or is culture at work? Ethnomusicologists, because of their ethnographic methods, are better at describing particular instances than at answering these general questions. But even if they tried, the phenomenon itself may be so variable and complex as to beggar generalization.

When observing these phenomena, it is tempting to assume that something in the music itself is causing the transformation from a normal to an altered state of being. In the 1960s the neurobiologist Andrew Neher published papers making this claim. Twenty years later the French ethnomusicologist Gilbert Rouget rebutted this idea in a comparative study of *Music and Trance*, which put the lie to causal explanations of the relation between music and trance. He documented "the disconcerting variability of the relation between music and the onset of trance." First, he argued that not all trance music is based on repeated, loud drum beats at a certain tempo or on repetitive melodic patterns, as Neher had suggested, although those are characteristics of a genre of popular electronic dance music called "trance music." Second, Rouget reasoned that if music were a direct cause of trance, then everyone at a music-trance event would go into trance. Actually only certain people go into trance, and the performing musicians almost never do. As Rouget put it, "Trance, as it is observed in possession cults, [is] a socialized form of behavior resulting from the conjunction of several constituents." In other words, the setting has to be right, the music has to be good, and the person or people going into trance have to be properly prepared. Sometimes, as among the Tumbuka of Malawi, trancers are special healers who have undergone training to be able to go into trance. In the spirit possession ceremonies (*bira*) of the Shona of Zimbabwe, trance ceremonies can last many hours as the musicians and participants seek the favorite tune of an ancestor and try to play it with enough energy to attract the ancestor to possess an adept.

It has proven almost impossible to understand the trance state from the point of view of the entranced, because they awaken with virtually no memory of it. What Rouget does conclude about the relation between music and trance is that although music may not cause trance, there is a very "stable relation to music. . . . It is due to the music, and because he is supported by the music, that the possessed person publicly lives out, by means of dance, his identification with the divinity he embodies." In a healing ritual called *vimbuza* among the Tumbuka people of Malawi, Steven Friedson has suggested that music creates a mental space where spirits can be "seen" and where "divination is enacted." Music does this by using a style with two organizations of beats (meters) at all times: the drum sounds may be structured in a 3+3 meter, while the hands are alternating in a 2+2+2 meter. Individuals choose which pattern or combination of patterns to bring into the foreground of consciousness and which to push into the background. Friedson concludes that

> [This] fluid polymorphous structure . . . is perhaps conducive to loosening up perceptual boundaries between object and subject. . . . The metrical doubling inherent in *vimbuza* drumming is mirrored, in a sense, in the consciousness-doubling of the healer's divinatory trance. . . . The same rhythmic figures that initially helped to bring on a total spirit possession now act as a kind of anchoring of consciousness, a focusing device that helps to stabilize the trance state and thus produce the doubling phenomenon.

This seems to be a specific instance of Rouget's notion that, while music may not cause the trance state, it can "support" it.

In an argument that combines culture and biology, Judith Becker claims that "deep listeners" who are profoundly moved, perhaps even to tears, by listening to Beethoven's "Moonlight Sonata" or John Lennon's "Imagine" could be similar to those who go into trance in religious or ritual contexts. She adds back the biological perspective that Rouget negated, seeking to find the sources of human emotional reactions to music in cognition. She acknowledges that, in order to enter a trance state, an individual must be socialized in the specific spiritual and ritual culture, and must be well versed in the expected outcome of the ritual or ceremony. Though she agrees that there may be no cross-cultural model for music-induced trance, she asserts that there are "limited universals" in trance experience such as emotional arousal, loss of a sense of self, cessation of inner language, and an extraordinary ability to withstand fatigue. Becker does not conflate deep listeners with religious trancers, but she links them by highlighting their similar emotional responses to musical stimuli. Whether Pentecostal worshippers, Balinese spirit-possession trancers, or deep listeners, she argues, they all have learned to regulate or modify cultural and biological systems of arousal to produce the same or similar physiological and neurological effects.

Claims for human universals in music making that rely on observed practices are few and far between. Recourse to a shared biology is potentially more fruitful, but it moves ethnomusicologists away from the lifeblood of their discipline, that is, ethnography grounded in intensive fieldwork in a particular culture, and the resulting claims about why people in a particular place and time make music in a particular way. However, such local studies do allow ethnomusicologists to make generalizations about the nature of music and to challenge those made by neurologists, biologists, and psychologists who fail to take human culture and particularity into account.

Chapter 6
Individual musicians

Ethnomusicologists work with exceptionally talented musicians in the course of their field research, but they do not, usually, fawn over the musical works and performances of great composers and performers. They do, however, argue that wonderful musicians exist in all societies. These musicians produce music of great intellectual, artistic, and cultural import worthy of scholarly attention for its own sake and for what it can tell us about why and how humans are musical. Rather than attributing a musician's skill to some inborn quality or supernatural gift like talent or genius, ethnomusicologists try to explain the social and cultural environment in which such skill and talent is developed and supported. They believe, in other words, that composers, compositions, performers, and performances participate in social and cultural systems. Still, despite ethnomusicologists' interest in the shared social and cultural life of music, they frequently write about individual musicians, some of them exceptional and some not so much.

Ethnomusicologists write about individuals partly as a matter of method. They realize that knowledge gained during research is not the product of objective observation but of particular interactions between individual fieldworkers and the individuals in a community with whom they work. This understanding of the research endeavor has led to some highly self-reflexive narratives that foreground not only the individual musicians being investigated but also the researcher herself. Also, ethnomusicologists have long felt uncomfortable that in their scholarly writing, they end up sounding like experts, when what they are doing is translating into ethnomusicological concepts the local knowledge of those they study, their "principal teachers," as Bruno Nettl has put it. And so they often name and quote extensively their sources, that is, the individuals who taught them about the music under investigation.

Other reasons for studying individuals have to do with theories of how culture works. Ethnomusicologists understand that individuals are not simply molded by culture and society but act as agents in the formation of musical cultures. Individuals are often credited with maintaining traditions through social and cultural action, and with changing traditions through the creation of new musical works and performances that respond to changes in the social and cultural life of the community.

One effect of these social changes is that individuals, in ever increasing numbers, are detaching themselves from their home communities. They are moving around the world because of the pull of new opportunities in richer lands or the push of war, famine, disease, and oppression in their homelands. Ethnomusicologists have found it fruitful to follow them and observe how they constitute new musical and social selves in new locations. For all these reasons, individuals of various types have long occupied a central role in ethnomusicological studies otherwise devoted to the study of music as culture.

Types of individuals

So what types of individuals do ethnomusicologists study? The compositional titans and stylistic innovators of European art music or the stars of popular music are not much in evidence in ethnomusicology, although there are important exceptions such as studies of the famous Egyptian singer Umm Kulthūm, the *salsa* king Tito Puente, and Afro-pop icon Fela Anikulapo-Kuti. Ethnomusicologists resist characterizing them as geniuses, however. Genius is a culturally constructed category, and it elevates certain individuals above culture and places them beyond the sphere of cultural explanation. Ethnomusicologists acknowledge their greatness but treat them as especially creative and noteworthy innovators or practitioners of a tradition. In addition to exceptional musicians and innovators, ethnomusicologists also take seriously and document the role of important figures in a tradition, of average musicians, and even of listeners, fans, producers, patrons, and club owners.

Ethnomusicological studies of musical innovators tend to take a historical approach, looking at music history as the product of agents changing musical practice in response to changing social conditions. They might focus on popular music, where the fame of named individuals and stars and their contributions to the history of a genre are the hallmarks of this musical domain; or they examine the encounter of a tradition with modern life, personified by an individual who articulates and acts on this key moment in the history of a tradition.

A study of innovators in the *conjunto* (small ensemble) tradition of so-called Tex-Mex music in southern Texas illustrates all three tendencies. Using historical and ethnographic methods, Manuel Peña has documented the individual innovators of *conjunto* music, played by a small ensemble of button accordion and *bajo sexto* (a twelve-string guitar). He positions them in the contexts of twentieth-century migration, urbanization, class differentiation, and identity formation. The first innovator, the accordionist and "father" of *conjunto* music, Narcisco Martinez, established the early instrumentation and melodic style of the genre between 1935 and 1940. After World War II, Valerio Longoria began singing lyrics to polka melodies and added a drum set to the ensemble. Tony de la Rosa electrified the bass and *bajo sexto*, gave microphones to the singers, and played in a more marcato style. This study is fairly typical of the approach to innovative individuals in ethnomusicology. Ethnomusicologists are not oblivious to the great innovators so lionized by historical musicology, but when they do treat individuals, they typically understand them as clever folks who responded more effectively or in a more timely fashion than others to the changing economic, political, and social circumstances in which they found themselves.

More frequent than studies of innovators are studies that focus on an important or key figure in a tradition. Perhaps they are extremely popular, or they occupy an important position in the tradition, or they are outstanding representatives of the style. Very often, the author of the study makes them into a key figure by placing them at the center of their narrative as a particular example of a general point the author wishes to make. I took this approach in a book I wrote , which chronicles the history of Bulgarian traditional music from the 1920s to 1989 by focusing on the musical experience of two key figures: Kostadin Varimezov (1918–2002) and his wife, Todora Varimezova (b. 1923). Kostadin occupied an important position in the official musical culture of Bulgaria during its communist period (1944–89) as the solo bagpiper in the orchestra of traditional Bulgarian instruments at the national radio station. His wife, Todora, was a key figure in the sense that she possessed an exceptionally large repertoire of traditional songs. This couple's grounding in traditional musical culture and their rich life experience in a village prior to World War II allowed me to narrate intimate stories about Bulgarian peasants' musical experience before their encounter with communism, industrialization, and urbanization. By focusing on Kostadin's transformation from a musically illiterate village player to a literate professional musician, and on Kostadin and Todora's musical lives in Bulgaria's capital city after World War II, I was able to humanize the more general story—one about Bulgarian musical culture in two distinct historical periods. Neither Kostadin nor Todora were innovators in the tradition, but I showed how their deep knowledge

7. Bulgarian bagpipe (*gaida*) player Kostadin Varimezov was a virtuoso village musician who learned to play an aural tradition in the 1930s. During the communist period (1944–89) he was trained to read music and became a soloist with the orchestra of folk instruments at the Bulgarian national radio.

of tradition made possible the innovations of others at the moment the Bulgarian musical tradition encountered modern life.

Ethnomusicologists are the products of a culture that values individual excellence and achievement, and by far the majority of their studies single out for attention outstanding musicians, whether innovators or key figures, for attention. However, a few have found it useful to pay attention to the average or ordinary musicians who are a part of every musical tradition. Harris Berger does this in his book about how musicians attend cognitively to music during performance. He studied a few small groups of journeyman jazz, rock, and heavy-metal musicians in the cities of Cleveland and Akron, Ohio. He sought to understand what the musicians focused on in order to create an engaging musical groove in each of these genres. When understanding and generalizing about typical individual musical experience is the point of the study, any individual will do, including unexceptional regional and local musicians crucial to the vitality of most every style of music.

Ethnomusicologists have long argued that listeners and others who participate as patrons, organizers, producers, and sound engineers should be considered musicians, and that they deserve to be studied as seriously as performers and composers. In fact, relatively few studies do this. One that does, by Lise Waxer (1965–2002), documents the role of a few entrepreneurs who created *salsotecas* in Cali, Colombia, in the 1980s. Live music and musicians working in dance clubs were associated with the wealth generated by the drug cartels. The owners of *salsotecas* played old recordings of *salsa* and helped to create an alliance between working-class people who couldn't afford the live-music clubs, and middle-class, educated, leftist intellectuals. The geographical distribution of these clubs mapped onto the class divisions of society. The DJs and the club aficionados spent a lot of time talking to Waxer about the music, treating *salsa* artists "as serious subjects of aesthetic and intellectual contemplation . . . [in order to] recuperate and keep alive Cali's musical history." This study's emphasis on club owners and their use of recordings to do social and cultural work is quite unusual in ethnomusicology.

Individuals and theories of culture

The last twenty years or so have seen a shift away from the search for the shared aspects of music culture toward the realization that cultures and societies are not happily homogenous but are often fragmented along lines of gender, social class, race, and ethnicity. The contestation of musical meaning across these social boundaries must be as true of culture as any claims about common, shared meanings and understandings. This relatively recent theoretical development has taken many forms. For example, ethnomusicologists tend to valorize individuality, individual skill differences, individual identity, and individual experience among musicians in a culture. They report on the differences and tensions that exist among individuals operating from different social and historical positions within a society. They construe individuals as agents who put into motion, give meaning to, and change social, cultural, and musical systems. And they foreground, in their narratives, the encounter between the ethnomusicologist and individuals in the field.

The valorization of individual difference and individual identity comes rather easily to ethnomusicologists, trained as most are in European traditions that value individuality in general and various forms of musical distinction in particular. Ethnomusicologists are eager to demonstrate, as Benjamin Brinner has for Javanese music, that musical knowledge varies within communities depending on "individual motivation and ability in response to community options and demands" and that "musicians do not know all aspects of a tradition to the same degree."

Ethnomusicologists also register the differences of interpretation and experience that result from stratification along the lines of age, social class, occupation, education, and urban versus rural residence. In a study of the pre-Hispanic Wanka people of the Mantaro Valley of Peru, Raúl Romero interpreted the contemporary *orquesta tipica* (ensemble of *quena* flute, violin, and harp) from three competing points of view: traditionalist, modernist, and radical. The traditionalist position was represented by an artist and intellectual who once resided in Europe, and who decried modernization and sought to preserve ancient practices. The modernist position was represented by a clarinet-playing music teacher who believed that modern instruments like the clarinet and the saxophone helped make traditional music sound better, and who claimed that modern music was more useful for creating cultural identity than the traditional forms were. The radical position was represented by younger musicians from ages fifteen to twenty-five who were experimenting with replacing the harp with the electric bass and the violin with the synthesizer. In this case, ideas about the value of different forms of music are not shared by a community, which is divided about how to deploy music most effectively as a cultural resource.

Ethnomusicologists nowadays typically understand musical individuals as agents who give meaning to—and change—social, cultural, and musical systems in specific instances. This position acts as a corrective to an earlier ethnomusicological theory that music and musicians merely reflect or participate in larger cultural and social processes. Virginia Danielson construed the Egyptian popular singer Umm Kulthūm as an agent of musical and cultural change. Kulthūm helped "constitute" cultural and social life, and "advance an ideology of Egyptianness" through musical choices that distanced her performance style from older Ottoman styles. Her music helped create a cultural and artistic world that was simultaneously Arab, European, and cosmopolitan—and in line with the nationalist politics of the period.

Finally, ethnomusicologists understand that the knowledge they generate about other musical cultures is not objective but is made possible by the conversations they have with those they meet in the field. As a consequence, they sometimes write not only about the individuals they meet but about themselves working in the field. In the process, they reflect on the social and cultural realities that form the background of the research enterprise. In a striking example, Katherine Hagedorn begins her book on the Afro-Cuban *santería* tradition with a literary account of a dream she had about one of the religious spirits she studied in Cuba. He appears frightening but does not harm her. She then spends most of the chapter positioning herself in relation to Cuban society: she was a woman learning a male tradition; she was white and most of her informants were black; she was well-off and they were poor; she was foreign and uninitiated in the religion. Her research conversations with individual musicians, including the distinguished drummer and leader Alberto Villareal, all took place against the background of these differences in social, political, economic, and racial positioning, and she makes those relationships an explicit part of her narrative throughout the book.

In some of the very earliest studies in ethnomusicology, individuals were largely absent in favor of reports on the general principles of musical style and its relationship to culture. Individuals began to appear in response to changes in theories of culture and in response to an increasing interest in the histories of traditions, outlined in chapter 7. In those histories, individuals often play a formative role.

Chapter 7
Writing music history

Although most ethnomusicologists are musical ethnographers who conduct fieldwork and write about the so-called ethnographic present, some are music historians who work principally with original manuscripts, previous publications, and recordings in libraries and archives. This is especially true of those working in East, Southeast, South, and West Asia, where there are long histories of music in written tradition. Even the musical ethnographers often spend a great deal of time recovering the history of the traditions they study, if they possibly can. They do so to understand how things got to be the way they are, why traditions change, and how people in the culture they study are constructing their own musical histories through their musical practices in the present.

Music histories

When ethnomusicologists write histories of music situated in a distant past, they do so in a way that makes it clear that historiography and ethnography are not very far apart. Joseph Lam, for example, draws from "standard documents" from the Ming dynasty, among them "Veritable Records of the Ming (Ming Shilu)," to write an account of *State Sacrifices and Music in Ming China (1368–1644)*. To compose this history, he consults musical notations from the Ming dynasty that he discovered in

1984 and that "preserve a large repertory of 322 state sacrificial songs." Using these documents, he creates a music history that echoes some contemporary themes in the writing of musical ethnographies, including contestation of values from multiple points of view and possibilities for individual expression in a highly structured environment. Ming dynasty ritual music was the result of a long series of negotiations involving court politics and struggles between officials and musicians. At issue, among other things, was a tension between creativity and orthodoxy. Rituals maintained their power and authority even as they became a vehicle for individual musicians to express themselves musically.

George Sawa draws extensively from two tenth-century Arabic-language sources, the *Kitab al-Musiqa al-Kabir* (Great Book of Music) and the *Kitab al-Aghani* (Book of Songs) to create an ethnomusicologically informed account of musical theory, practice, and life in Baghdad, Damascus, Mecca, and Isfahan in that period. He is also able, with his extensive knowledge of contemporary Arab musical practice, to provide detailed translations of the musical theory in the Great Book of Music, in a sense doing music history backwards, that is, using the present to inform the understanding of an account from the past.

In both these examples and many others, ethnomusicologists writing music history do so in a way that emphasizes ethnomusicological themes, questions, and values.

Modern music history

More typical of ethnomusicology than studies of music set completely in the distant past are those concerned with what has been called "modern music history" written from a perspective called "historical ethnomusicology." In these studies the history of music begins within the "ethnographic present," the time horizon accessible to synchronic fieldwork. They then work backward in time from there. In such settings, ethnomusicologists learn of distinctions

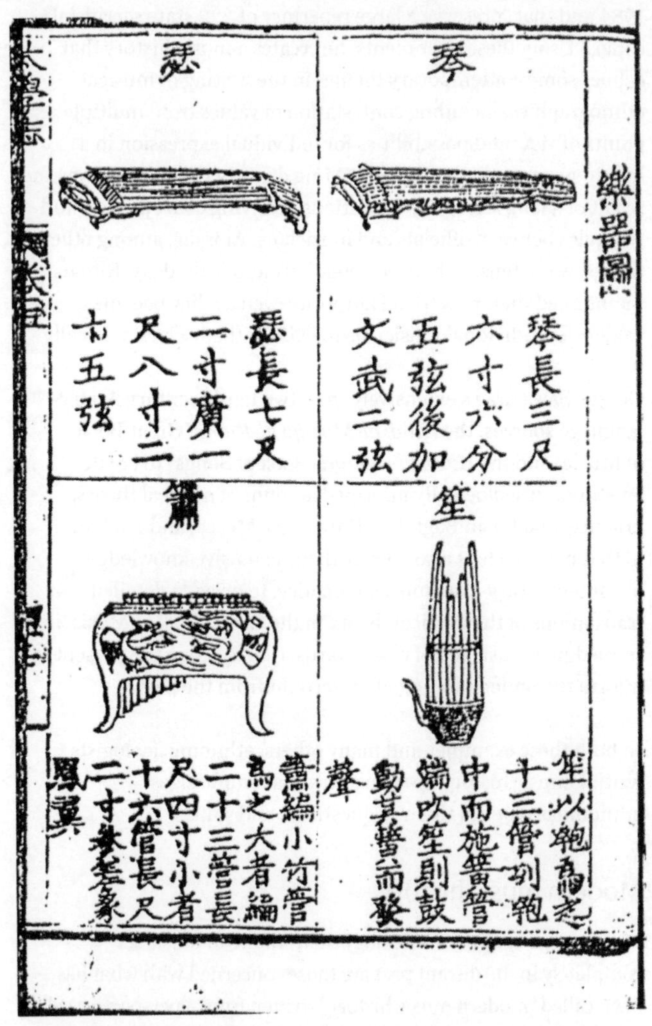

8. The *Huang Ming taixue ji* (Records of the imperial university of the Ming, 1556) contains this set of four drawings of Chinese musical instruments: clockwise from *upper left*, twenty-five-string zither (*se*), seven-string zither (*qin*), mouth organ (*sheng*), and panpipe (*paixiao*).

people make between older and newer forms of music. They then write histories, using historical writings and recordings when they are available, which place each kind of music in its particular cultural context. They explain the reasons behind the emergence of the newer forms and the fate of the older forms. They excavate the past to illuminate the present life of a musical tradition, and they show how people in the culture construct their own music histories.

During ethnomusicology's early period, the study of modern music history was often framed as the study of musical change within a worldview that valued traditional music. In this paradigm the stability of tradition was taken for granted as natural, and change was a problem to be explained. Was it the result of culture contact? A desire to revitalize the fading significance of tradition in the face of modern life and contact with European culture? A creative individual engagement with the artistic possibilities of hybridization and fusion of musical styles?

Some of the earliest studies along this line concerned culture contact in the New World between European colonizers, their slaves, and indigenous populations. Borrowing from religious studies, these ethnomusicologists used the term "syncretism" to explain the musical forms of enslaved Africans and their descendents, notably the song-and-drumming traditions associated with new religious practices, which "syncretized" or fused elements of Catholicism with West African animist religions. Over time, the African polyrhythms of these syncretic musical styles combined with European-derived melodies and harmonies to create the huge variety of popular and folk traditions in Latin America today. An early theory of how this happened posited similarities of musical style as a determining factor. An often-cited example is the Cuban and Mexican *son* traditions, song genres that preserve a polymetric feel that alternates between 6/8 and 3/4: 3+3 and 2+2+2. This metric ambiguity was a feature of both African and Spanish music at the time the cultures came in contact in the sixteenth and seventeenth centuries.

Beyond musical similarities, the fusion of African with European music took different forms in Latin America and in North America. Ethnomusicologists usually explain this difference between musical syncretism in North and South America in terms of cultural differences. The Roman Catholic church in Latin America allowed syncretism in theology and music as a path to conversion, while North American Protestants forbade pagan African practices and the drums and music that went along with them, forcing the expression of Africanisms into new musical channels such as spirituals and worksongs, and later jazz and gospel hymns.

Studies in the last thirty years have tended to regard both change and stability as natural to a musical culture, and both are in need of explanation. Instead of viewing change as a symptom of decline or a lamentable concession to the forces of modernization and Europeanization, recent historical narratives suggest that cultures have always been dynamic and in contact with other cultures. People have always treated their musical traditions inventively and strategically as resources to revitalize their communities, cope with devastation and change, make older forms of music meaningful in new social and cultural environments, and move toward a hopeful future.

More often studied these days than culture contact are instances of change within cultures and societies, especially as they, along with their musical traditions, encounter rural to urban migration, universal education, industrialization and capitalism, ideologies such as nationalism and communism, and globalization in the form of massive flows of people, ideas, money, mediated symbolic forms, and technology. In these cases factors other than musical similarities seem to be at work, such as the interplay between the powerful and powerless, the creativity of individuals, and the effect on music of specific instances of cultural, social, political, or economic change.

Ethnomusicologists tend to suppose that when cultural, social, political, or economic systems change, some aspects of musical practice and style will change as a consequence. Old musical forms may diminish in importance, continue—but with new cultural meanings assigned to them, change to meet new demands, or be abandoned altogether. When none of the old forms are adequate to new social and cultural demands, then new forms of music will almost surely be invented to meet new needs. During the 1950s, for example, the civil rights movement among African Americans in the United States created a new sense of optimism among Blacks that they could "move on up" and into equality with White Americans. The new cultural and political world they were creating revealed a problem with the community's principal musical genres, those of gospel and blues. The blues generally portrayed a secular life of defeat in personal terms while gospel held out the hope of salvation in the afterlife and release from a world of woes. Neither addressed the new optimism and hope for freedom from oppression in this world. In such a situation ethnomusicologists would expect a new genre to emerge and one did: soul music. The stars of the new genre, Ray Charles, Aretha Franklin, and James Brown, had deep roots in church music, and they melded the optimistic tone of gospel music to new texts proclaiming Black Pride and successful personal relationships: "I Got a Woman"; "Respect"; "Say It Loud, I'm Black and I'm Proud." In this context blues as a genre diminished in importance for the Black community, although its stylistic gestures continue to infuse jazz, soul, and gospel. Instead, blues in the 1960s became a favorite form of White American and British musicians, who lionized traditional blues singers and built their rock music on a blues base. The alienation that the blues expressed seemed a perfect match for the anger and angst that White youth felt and needed to express during the Vietnam War era.

Sometimes social and political change causes old musical forms to change so that new meanings can be assigned to them. In the former Yugoslavia, for example, a genre of popular music called "newly composed folk music" emerged in the 1960s. According to Ljerka Rasmussen, this genre expressed a necessary cultural middle ground between the rural "folk" and the urban high-brow, as well as a sense of Yugoslavia as a modern, Europeanizing state. When Yugoslavia dissolved into war among its federated states in the early 1990s, the genre's link to a Yugoslav sensibility was severed, and elements of its style shifted to express nationalist identities: Serbians accompanied the songs with the accordion typical of their "folk music"; Croatians with their "national" instrument, the *tamburitsa*; and Bosnian Muslims with Ottoman-derived long-necked lutes. Within Serbia the genre, rechristened "turbofolk," became a symbol of Slobodan Milošević's oppressive, nationalist regime, and so the music was either loved by his supporters or reviled by those who opposed his excesses.

Contemporary culture places new demands on traditional forms of music the world over. Sometimes musicians, scholars, and governments take an active interest in changing music to meet new demands. Sometimes the music seems to change as an unintended consequence of, for example, its institutionalization. In one case, scholars intervened to try to change a musical tradition as a response to modernization. Middle Eastern music (Arab, Turkish, and Persian) is notable for its use of microtonal intervals. At a famous conference of Middle Eastern and European scholars in Cairo in 1932, some tried to articulate new, more modern practices for the tradition. The ethnomusicologist A. J. Racy writes, "In the deliberations of the Committee for Modes and Composition, some Egyptian members passionately advocated the use of the equal-tempered scale of twenty-four quarter-tones," making an analogy to the "modern" European system of twelve equal-tempered half steps. "The two Turkish participants, however, rejected the quarter-tone system on account of its arbitrary nature and inappropriateness for the accurate measurement of Near Eastern pitch." The congress seemed to have had a negligible effect on performance practice, although "the idea of introducing quarter-tone keyboard instruments has by no means died out."

In Bulgaria during its communist era from 1944 to 1989, the intelligentsia appropriated Bulgarian rural music as a symbol of national identity. But to make it a suitable emblem of its progressive ideas about the future of humankind under communism, classically trained composers took traditional melodies and rhythms, originally performed solo or in small groups, and "arranged" and "refined" them for performances by large choruses and orchestras of folk instruments using European tonal harmonies and countrapuntal textures.

One force for musical change in nation-states that use music as a symbol of national identity has been the institutionalization of music, particularly the formation of conservatories of traditional music and folkloric performance ensembles. Judith Becker claimed that when a conservatory of music was formed in Indonesia and students were trained using musical notation rather than by traditional aural methods, variation and improvisation disappeared in favor of the performance of "correct" versions of pieces.

In the face of urbanization and industrialization, people sometimes abandon musical genres and practices. In Europe, for example, as older occupations, patterns of life, and agrarian magical belief systems disappeared, the songs associated with them either ceased to be sung or are today performed by newly created folklore ensembles and in festivals, where they become a genre (harvest song, shoemaker's song) whose performance generates memories of, and nostalgia for, an older, long gone, practice.

Another form of theorizing about the causes of musical change flows from the claim that music's particular form and effects depend on its means of production. One of the clearest examples of this Marxist position is Peter Manuel's study of "cassette culture" in India. In the late 1970s, a small handful of filmmakers and musical performers promoted a standardized, common-denominator approach to musical products that were communicated unidirectionally from corporations to a consuming audience. With the rise of audio cassettes as a means of production, the equipment to produce recordings was inexpensive to acquire and easy to use. It facilitated the decentralized, grassroots control of a significant sector of the mass media. The spread of cassette production stimulated a revival of interest in "traditional" regional music. It spurred syncretism between genres and the formation of new musical forms, and it allowed the presentation and negotiation of local identities within smaller regional spheres.

Sometimes the outward forms of music remain largely unchanged, but the meaning of the form changes in new contexts. According to Philip Bohlman, this happened with classical Viennese chamber music performed by Central European Jews. In Europe, the playing of string quartets and other forms of chamber music in house concerts was one way for Jews "to enter European traditions of civilization, thus coupling their own history to another." When these Jewish musicians immigrated to Israel, their continued performances sustained long-cherished cultural values of education and helped to create a subgroup known as *Yekkes*. The group is, in some ways, "a product of its musical activities," and, along with other boundary markers such as speaking German and wearing jackets (*yekkes*) in hot weather, has some of the features of an ethnic group within the diversity of Israeli society. As Bohlman points out, such a particular history of a European musical genre can challenge the status of a single, monolithic history of European music. The existence of multiple histories speaks to the cultural values people attach to what is usually construed as a unitary tradition of "absolute music."

Alan Lomax famously worried that modernization would result in a "cultural gray-out" that would bleach the vibrant mosaic of musics that humankind has created. In fact, the record has been mixed. Faced with the pressure to modernize, people have often turned old musical forms to new purposes, in the process making the color vibrant for a new age. But some genres have been lost or their importance reduced and, even when the genre is not lost, key elements of its style may have changed. Even as ethnomusicologists report enthusiastically on the continued vitality of older styles and the emergence of new ones, David Coplan believes that at least some "are to some degree concerned by the retreat of genuinely non-European music and musicians into dwindling, ever more remote areas, and by traditional music's loss of currency and involvement in the actual daily life of so many of the world's peoples."

Perhaps ethnomusicologists' unavoidable engagement with history and change as they study music ethnographically and synchronically is the reason Bruno Nettl suggested that the field might be defined as the "science of music history" and suggested that its "value and contribution . . . seem to me to be essentially and very broadly historical."

Chapter 8
Ethnomusicology in the modern world

Once upon a time, ethnomusicologists studied primarily "traditional music." Many expressed their aversion to the study of popular, commercial, and urban musics and to neotraditional music tainted by supposedly inauthentic modern performance contexts such as folkloric ensembles, radio and television broadcasts, conservatories of music, Christian missions, and tourism sites. Today these reservations have been completely erased, and ethnomusicologists are busily studying every kind of music they encounter in the world, including American popular music, European art music, local and ethnic forms of popular music, Christian music in postmissionary settings, music for tourists, music that supports or resists totalitarian regimes, and on and on. If ethnomusicologists once championed ostensibly pure forms of traditional music, today they revel in the musical hybridity, fusion, deconstruction, and bricolage that musicians everywhere are deploying to make sense of the modern, globalized, spatially unbounded, unstable, frequently painful world of endless possibilities in which they live, work, travel, and make music.

Globalization and popular music

Ethnomusicologists once acted as if they made a radical distinction between themselves as modern and cosmopolitan and those they studied as traditional and local. They went in search of "authentic" and perhaps ancient musical expressions of premodern culture and society, and eschewed new, arranged, "folklorized," planned interventions ("fakelore" some called it) by nation-states, tourism entrepreneurs, and other modern institutions. In the late 1960s and early 1970s, I bypassed Bulgaria's communist-era "national ensembles" of folk music, song, and dance, with their choreographies, orchestras and choruses, conductors, and European harmonies and counterpoints, and headed to villages where I looked for what I imagined to be ancient, exotic, unique ways of making music. I hoped to document and understand part of the record of human musical diversity.

It did not take long for ethnomusicologists to realize that modern life had come to many of the local cultures we studied long before we arrived in the field, whether in the form of Spanish and Portuguese colonization in the New World in the 1600s, the arrival of U.S. Admiral Matthew Perry's squadron in Japan in the 1850s, or communist totalitarianism in the 1900s. Ethnomusicologists were soon studying musical forms created in the blending of indigenous, African, and European cultures in Latin America, saxophones in Cantonese opera orchestras, Highlife dance music in urban West Africa, compositions for the Japanese *koto* (zither) by Michio Miyagi(1894–1956), and reggae and dub in Jamaica.

Ethnomusicologists today have largely abandoned their construction of the world in two spheres—the traditional and the modern. They have, instead, become completely engaged with the mixing, hybridization, and syncretism of musical forms that arguably began along the ancient silk road, became a fact of life in the wake of European colonialism, and has reached unprecedented proportions with the capitalist penetration of world and local markets, and the commodification of labor and social relationships. Today, the ease of travel, the migration of people from villages to cities, the emigration of people from troubled lands, and readily available technology to share ideas and cultural artifacts across vast spaces help configure musical processes in nearly every part of the globe.

Ethnomusicologists study not only the new hybrid forms that occur in these conditions but also how local musicians use them to advance personal and social agendas, and to resist the social and cultural destruction that can accompany these flows of goods, services, people, and ideas. Globalization has created wildly disparate economic advantages and disadvantages for individuals and groups in particular local circumstances. Ethnomusicologists worry that commodification, coupled with the vast difference in wealth between the West and the rest, disempowers local musicians and may result in the disappearance of noncommodifiable musical practices. On the other hand, globalization and its accompanying spatial, economic, and ideational disruptions call into question, threaten, and require a healing musical response to crises of personal and social identity.

Musical production in these contexts can be a helpful way to deal with the psychological and social ruptures caused by separation from older ways of being and by expanded social interactions with people in cities, new countries, or over the Internet. Steven Feld has written that

> Musical globalization is experienced and narrated as equally celebratory and contentious because everyone can hear equally omnipresent signs of augmented and diminished musical diversity. Tensions around the meanings of sonic heterogeneity and homogeneity precisely parallel other tensions that characterize global processes of separation and mixing.

While some ethnomusicologists worry about the homogenizing effects of globalization, others celebrate local musicians' capacity to respond creatively to the disruptive effects of globalization.

Another matter altogether is commercial world music created by Euro-American artists such as Paul Simon, Peter Gabriel, Deep Forest, Ry Cooder, and others, who have been criticized as exploitative because of differences in economic wealth and symbolic capital between these musicians and the local artists with whom they work. For example, Paul Simon's albums, at least the ones that depend on the musicians and musical styles of South Africa and Brazil, have created a double-edged sword: money, power, prestige, and copyright rest with Simon, while the local musicians share principally in the reflected glory, which they can use to their advantage locally and in subsequent world tours, where they can make a bit of money. While Simon would surely characterize his appropriation of these styles as an act of admiration and respect, Feld worries that his "melody" is "harmonized by a counter-melody" of power, domination, and control:

> All of the performance styles (the grooves, beats, sounds, genres) are South African in makeup (whatever influences they synthesize and incorporate). While the contribution of Simon's lyrics is clear and important, the contribution of the music, its unique and distinct and formative influence on the quality and particularity of the record, is clearly downplayed.

Examining Simon's *Graceland* as a cultural product, Louise Meintjes, originally from South Africa, published a multilayered analysis of this album and its local effects and interpretations. Among Black South Africans, some argued that international exposure to Black South African music and musical styles was a sign of high value being placed on African music. Others worried that such commodification of their traditions risked erasing those sounds as signs of community. Those in the liberation movement thought that international cooperation at that fraught moment in history might confuse people about the nature of their resistance to apartheid. White South Africans interpreted *Graceland* differently, as well. Conservatives saw Simon's effort as an "improvement" on

African expressions and a challenge to the "silliness" of the cultural sanctions imposed on South Africa. Liberals saw it as a "gateway to the future" and a sign of respect for African musical forms. Meintjes's study delineates the local tensions brought to light, addressed, worked out, and given emotional power through the creation of hybrid musical forms.

Although the work of European stars like Simon may grab most of the public attention, ethnomusicologists are increasingly documenting how immigrant musicians in metropoles around the world are creating new works in the commercial category of world music. These immigrants often feel disconnected from their homeland but not yet connected to, and even marginalized in, their new homeland. There, they have access to a vast array of musics and musicians from which to fashion a new self through a new musical style based on fusion, syncretism, hybridization, creolization, and pastiche. These new, personal musical styles, if successful, speak to a whole community and beyond, to a world of fans seeking new renditions of something they imagine to be traditional and authentic. In his book *Global Pop,* Timothy Taylor profiles some of these artists living in Paris, London, Africa, and South Asia, including two Anglo-Asians: Sheila Chandra and a man who took the *nom de musique* "Apache Indian." Chandra, for example, imagines a kind of global consciousness in which similarities of musical style are more important than musical differences. She rejects a fusion of Indian music with European music in favor of a belief that musicians from all over the world can sing in her "ancestors' voices": "I believe that my heritage comes not specifically from my own culture. I believe I am a spiritual heir to a universal form of inspiration." The result, predictably, has a vaguely indistinct, new-age quality. Apache Indian, on the other hand, imagines a new self and a new music born of the combination of the Punjabi popular-music genre *bhangra* and Jamaican reggae. He grew up with both musics in his ears and combined them to express a sense of self that was an amalgam of these two worlds: "Regardless of what anybody said [about reggae], it was for me."

Today ethnomusicologists routinely study not only these international syntheses but local versions of Anglo-American pop, rock, and rap, and the cultural work they do. A short list gives a sense of the range of music being covered: the extreme metal scene in Brazil; Balinese death/thrash metal; hip-hop in Istanbul; Burmese rap; punk in China; and rock music among Tibetans exiled in Dharamsala, India.

When ethnomusicologists turn their attention to American popular music, they run into a problem created by their ethnographic method. Although they can conduct fieldwork among fans, producers, club owners, and unknown musicians and bands, the stars of the genre usually refuse to be studied, fearing, reasonably enough, that there is nothing in it for them except unwanted critical scrutiny. If ethnomusicologists do write about pop stars, they are often forced to fall back on archival research, analysis of recordings, and reading interviews by journalists, all respectable research methods but a bit distant from their interest in encountering their sources directly, and reporting on intentionality and meaning from the perspective of the makers of musical traditions.

Music, media, and technology

Recently, a colleague who teaches a course on fieldwork methods in ethnomusicology reported that the students reacted to her lessons on audio recording techniques in the field with indifference and even disdain. They pointed out that they would not be studying live musical performances, as she had; they would be studying traditions already made in recording studios and released on commercial recordings. There was no need, they contended, to make live recordings of the traditions that interested them; they were already recorded. This anecdote signals a real shift in the work of ethnomusicologists, who once tended (and some still do) to regard live performance as the source of, and therefore more "authentic" than, recorded performances. Or, they might argue, live performance is better able to contribute to face-to-face community building than the mediated construction of imagined communities of fans and affinity groups sharing a dehumanized, "schizophonic" (sound makers separated from their sounds) musical experience in far-flung places. Today, ethnomusicologists rarely encounter music that has not been mediated in some way, and they recognize the extent to which listening to recordings has become, in many parts of the world, people's principal experience of music.

The recognition of the importance of media and technology, not simply as a means of recording live music but as a fundamental fact of modern musical life, has led to the study of what René Lysloff terms music and "technoculture." Arguing that "the ethnographic Other is now fully plugged in," he suggests that ethnomusicologists examine the cultural use of musical technology as seriously as they study unmediated performances. Many interesting questions arise: How do the musical communities formed by using technology differ in their use and experience of music from communities formed by physical proximity or shared cultural heritage? What are the effects of technology on musical memory? How do recordings change our ideas of what is "authentic" and "real" in music? How are recordings and other media put in the service of reflexive projects such as the construction of individual and social identities? How are relationships of power and authority enacted in mediated performances and their distribution? How do recordings expand or contract the audiences and the incomes of traditional musicians? Answering these questions has led to new orientations toward, and locales for, fieldwork.

A now-common topic concerns the introduction of electronic musical instruments into traditional ensembles and performance, usually to make them sound more modern while retaining something of their original meaning. Lysloff reports that "in Javanese shadow theater performances in the region of Banyumas, musicians sometimes use a Casio keyboard in addition to the gamelan, for creating sound effects to accompany action scenes." A popular music genre, *dangdut*, "featuring an Indian tabla-like sound" is transformed into *disco-dangdut* through the introduction of "sampled sounds and high-tech musical instruments [and] a faster beat."

Some have worked on how people deploy musical products like LP records, audio cassettes, and CDs and their attendant playback technologies to create live performances, music scenes, or new recordings, techniques that are the lifeblood of hip-hop, Jamaican dub, and electronic dance music of all sorts. A pioneering effort in this regard was Charles Keil's 1984 study of karaoke in Japan, just as dub in Jamaica and rap in the United States burst on the scene. Keil commented,

> What is striking to me in all these instances of mediated and live musical performances is first of all the humanizing or, better still, personalization of mechanical processes. . . . Perhaps it gives people a sense of reclaiming the music from the record companies and their machinery. Adding a "rap" or mixing the prerecorded tracks differently in "dub" puts the individual back in control of the processor or at least gives the illusion of such control.

Some ethnomusicologists have taken on parts of the music industry, including record companies, radio, magazines, and music publishing as sites for research. Recording studios are particularly fruitful fieldwork sites because of the musical and cultural work that goes on there. Louise Meintjes's study of "the politics of Zulu music production in the South African music industry in the early 1990s" shows how mixing in the studio includes the "negotiation for control over the electronic manipulation of style" and the creation of musical signs of "Otherness, Africanness, and Zuluness."

The Internet, websites, and services like iTunes, Pandora, Facebook, MySpace, and online games are potential sites for community formation, and ethnomusicologists are beginning to study them. William Cheng employed virtual and real fieldwork to understand a virtual gaming community in which players in a multiplayer game called *The Lord of the Rings Online* used "music to sound out alternative identities and to forge social ties in a dynamic role-playing universe."

Music, health, and healing

Ethnomusicologists have long been interested in the relationship between music, illness, and healing. Until recently these have taken the form of local ethnographic studies in cultures that believe in the power of music to cure illnesses, particularly illnesses that are attributed to supernatural causes. Most local explanations of music's efficacy depend on, and embed music within, the logic of deep cosmologies. Some ethnomusicologists are searching for medical explanations of these phenomena. In a study of a healing ritual in the Pamir Mountains of Tajikistan, Benjamin Koen's measurements of changes in heart-rate and blood pressure showed that devotional music lowered blood pressure and presumably stress, a finding that suggests that integration of physiological experiments with musical ethnography may be fruitful.

Other ethnomusicologists have turned their attention to what role music might play in dealing with health issues in the modern world, in particular the HIV/AIDS pandemic and the apparent increase in cases of Autism Spectrum Disorder (ASD) in the United States. In the latter case, ethnomusicologists are working with medical professionals to document the musical effects they observe when they perform music with and for children with ASD. In one study Michael Bakan and his colleagues used world-music instruments to animate improvisatory musical play among children and adults. They found that children who participated in this highly individualized program showed improved ability to connect socially on and beyond the music playground, and were able to transfer their musical experiences back into their home and school environments.

In the case of HIV/AIDS music has been employed principally to educate people about the clinical reality of the disease in parts of eastern and southern Africa where public policy and cultural ideologies sometimes combine to obfuscate the causes of the disease and deceive people into ignoring safe sexual practices. Gregory Barz reports that songs have been utilized in Uganda to deal with HIV/AIDS in health education, biomedical interventions, promotion of communication about disease, and the loss of cultural memory when an entire generation is decimated. Advocates for the ability of music to heal or to ameliorate illness and its causes have dubbed this emerging subfield "medical ethnomusicology," a praxis joining music, medicine, other healing arts, social action, and the study of culture.

War, violence, and conflict

Perhaps because ethnomusicologists for so long focused on traditional music in stable settings of communal performance or institutional patronage, they have been rather slow, compared with their colleagues in anthropology, to deal with the severe problems facing people around the world. Only since the late 1990s have ethnomusicologists fully engaged with questions of music's role in ameliorating or exacerbating the wars, violence, and conflict facing so many of the world's people today.

Among the first to do so were ethnomusicologists living in worn-torn areas. Croatian scholars caught in the horrible, ethnic-cleansing wars attending the breakup of Yugoslavia in the 1990s published a heartfelt collection of essays called *Music, Politics, and War: Views from Croatia*. Americans endured their own local experience of war on September 11, 2001, which stimulated a collection of essays titled *Music in the Post-9/11 World*.

Working in war zones, postwar zones, and other places of violence, conflict, and profound loss has led many ethnomusicologists to design or participate in practical projects to heal the wounds of loss and separation, and improve relations between communities in conflict. Croatian ethnomusicologist Svanibor Pettan, for example, designed CDs, films, and other publications less for an academic audience than to educate policy makers about the plight of Roma musicians displaced by the war between Serbs and Albanians in Kosovo. He also worked in Norway to create musical bridges between Bosnian refugees and Norwegians through shared musical performances of Bosnian repertoire. He wanted to help Bosnians feel proud of their identity and help the Norwegians understand better a minority in their midst.

One of the sobering realizations brought to the fore in these studies is that groups in conflict often use music to shut out, antagonize, exacerbate differences from, and even terrorize Others, while ethnomusicologists and those favoring peace generally believe that music is an ideal expressive form for conflict resolution, intercultural understanding, and healing. In Northern Ireland, during the "Troubles" between Catholic Republicans and Protestant Unionists from the 1960s to the 1990s, Protestants emphasized differences in what was once arguably a shared tradition. Some Unionists rejected Irish musical traditions as "alien" and instead valorized "Scottish" folk music or a constructed "Ulster-Scots" tradition. Protestant extremists used loud fife-and-drum bands to mark space as their own on certain holidays, throwing music in the faces and ears of those they opposed and terrorizing them with their loud iconic threats of military-style violence.

This example and newer ones from the battlefields of Afghanistan and Iraq and the interrogation rooms of the so-called war on terror illustrate how music can be used, according to John O'Connell, "to incite terror in the hearts of the dispossessed." However, it is much more common for ethnomusicologists to find examples, like Salwa Castelo-Branco does, where music provides "a platform for dialogue among factions in strife, relaxing tensions, stimulating communal feelings, expressing solidarity, reducing conflict, ultimately leading to reconciliation and peace." Anthony Seeger has described how

9. The aggressive music of bands of fifes and Lambeg drums, like this one marching in a parade in the town of Ballymena in Northern Ireland, often supported extreme Protestant loyalists during the conflict with Catholic Republicans from the late 1960s to 1998.

music created a peaceful mediation between Brazilians and the Suyá Indians of the Amazonian basin when they first contacted one another in 1959. The Suyá, who heard the nonmusical sounds of the Brazilians' boat engines as threatening, might have attacked them using silence, whispers, and shouts in their own language as sonic tools. Instead, realizing they were vastly outnumbered and doomed to defeat, they engaged the Brazilians with music and dance performances, expressive forms not requiring mutual linguistic understanding. Faced with these performances, the Brazilians also rejected violence and sang songs with guitar accompaniments for the Suyá. Music and dance, organized in rhythmic and melodic unison, and reciprocal listening provided icons of the proper functioning of social relationships. When the Suyá sang for the Brazilians, it "was the opposite of attacking them and was an expression of [their] peaceful intentions."

Finally, there have been a few studies of music in countries completely devastated by war. In Afghanistan, the Soviet occupation of the country in 1978 initiated a long period of conflict, which has lasted to the present. Many musicians have been killed while others have fled to the neighboring countries of Pakistan and Iran or to Europe, the United States, and Australia. Music schools, universities, and the national radio station have been severely weakened. Songs that before 1978 were principally about various forms of romantic, mystical, and patriotic love were politicized by the communists and the opposition mujahideen, banned by the Taliban, and transformed by Islamists into laments and tales of heroism. In 2005 no female singers were being trained, and teachers of any form of music were hard to find, because so many musicians had emigrated. Clearly these armed conflicts have been devastating and need to end before, as Veronica Doubleday puts it, "Afghanistan's remarkable musical culture [can] regenerate fully and flower again."

Climate change

The study of music in its relation to culture and society has also led some ethnomusicologists to embed their studies of music in a larger world of sonic experience. They have examined the boundaries between speech and song; the effect of tonal languages in Africa and China on melodic patterning; the way poetic meter affects musical rhythm; the relationship between speaking style and musical style; appropriate moments for talking, singing, and remaining silent; and the relationship between music and the environment.

The last topic is inspired in no small part by Canadian composer R. Murray Schafer and his World Soundscape Project. Calling his work "acoustic ecology," he challenged musicians to hear the "soundscape" as a composition for which they bear some ethical responsibility. Partly as a result, an enlarged domain of "sound studies" is currently emerging around the edges of ethnomusicology. Steven Feld has been one of its leaders, coining the term "acoustemology" to capture the notion that anthropologists and ethnomusicologists need to understand a culture's sonic epistemology, their way of knowing the world through its sounds, in balance with its way of knowing the world visually and verbally. This phenomenon is often characterized as directly physical and therefore emotional; as deeply connected to the experience of "truth"; as a supplement to now-standard accounts of music's meaning and reference to a social and cultural world; and as a way to bring attention in sound and music studies to sensation over representation, emotion over meaning, and aurality and physicality over literacy and reflection.

Tina Ramnarine, for example, describes the acoustemology of the Sámi of northern Europe, an indigenous nomadic people famous as reindeer herders. They perform a genre called *joiking* (vocalizing with "irregular phrasing . . . a distinctive vocal timbre . . . and rising microtonal pitches"). They believe that they can *joik* people, landscapes, and animals into existence, in the process placing themselves discursively in the environment rather than in relationship to it, a way of talking about the human-nature relationship rather different from familiar European ones. In his 1993 *Bird Symphony* Nils-Aslak Valkeapää (1943–2001), a Sámi composer, poet, and activist, placed *joiks* within a recorded soundscape of birdsong, water sounds, and reindeer bells. He wanted to express the unity of man and nature, and to call attention to indigenous concerns about the degradation of the polar environment due to climate change, nuclear-waste dumping, and logging. Other Sámi composers have placed *joiks* in a sound environment that includes snowmobiles and other machines as a way of engaging critically with their emerging actual soundscape, not with a mythical, idealized, "natural" past. These new Sámi compositions, in harmony with the newly noisy polar soundscape, challenge "the notion that sound mediates between humans and their environments, inviting us instead to consider human musical creativity situated within sonic ecosystems and across species-boundaries," and opening up the possibility for what Ramnarine calls "environmental ethnomusicology."

Nancy Guy worries that ethnomusicologists may be ignoring the single greatest crisis of our time, climate change, and argues for adopting an "ecocritical" sensibility. Her project documents the references in Taiwanese popular song to nature, particularly to the Tamsui River, which runs near Taipei. Before World War II, popular song lyrics evoked its beauty in narratives of human love and affection for the river itself. After the war, references to the river disappeared as immigration of mainland Chinese and rapid industrialization turned it into a polluted nightmare that needed to be cut off from view with high walls. Such songs were no longer relevant in a world that valorized growth and development at the expense of the physical world. This changed again in the 1980s when the river returned as the focus of songs critical of environmental degradation. Her vision of an "ecomusicology" leads her to ask whether music may be a resource that can "contribute to our survival" or whether it is indifferent to our species' possible extinction.

Whether it involves globalization and popular music; music media and technology; pandemic diseases; war, violence, and conflict; or climate change, ethnomusicologists today engage with the full range and richness of human music making the world over, not least because so many people in the modern world seem to believe that music is indeed a matter of life and death.

Chapter 9
Ethnomusicologists at work

Most very short introductions to academic disciplines assume them to be, well, academic. Disciplines are about the life of the mind in a particular domain supported by universities, research institutes, governments, and, in the case of the sciences, private industry. Ethnomusicology is a bit different in this regard. It has always been on the margins of music studies, struggling for a seat at the master's table, as it were. And, because ethnomusicologists work with human beings, they have always been concerned about the ethical implications of their work and what responsibilities they have to the people with whom they conduct research. So the question of where ethnomusicologists work, and what kind of work they do, has long occupied a central place in their thinking about the field.

To flourish, academic disciplines must be supported by societies and institutions that find their research potentially valuable. Scholars, in turn, must contribute their newly discovered knowledge to society, whether in the abstract, as an addition to knowledge, or in its practical application to society's problems. Finding institutional support for ethnomusicology has been somewhat problematic because its advocacy of a global perspective on music and its belief in the equal human value of all music challenge widely held notions, supported by powerful institutions, that value in music is defined by the supposed aesthetic superiority of European art music or by its commercial potential. In these contexts, the question of which institutions support ethnomusicology and where ethnomusicologists work takes on special importance in a very short introduction to the field.

University homes

When ethnomusicology's founders decided to form the new Society for Ethnomusicology and not to work within the long-established American Musicological Society or the American Anthropological Association, their decision undoubtedly helped to foster a vigorous new discipline. With its new name and a strong sense of difference from its forebears, ethnomusicology has struggled mightily ever since to find an institutional home within English-speaking universities.

Although it has evolved over the years into a field perhaps well described as the anthropology of music, it has largely failed to find a home in departments of anthropology with a few exceptions: Alan Merriam trained some students at Indiana University; and John Blacking developed a program at Queen's University, Belfast. Martin Stokes suggested a plausible reason for this:

> In accordance with the highly pervasive fiction of an earlier musicology, music is still . . . considered [by anthropologists] a domain of a special, almost extra-social, autonomous experience. What ethnomusicologists deal with in the societies they study is—anthropologists are residually inclined to assume—either the diversionary or the arcane. By definition they cannot be dealing with the kinds of events and processes that make up the predominantly verbal and visual "real life" of which social reality is assumed to consist.

By far the most welcoming home for ethnomusicology has proven to be departments and schools of music. Historically, such departments focused exclusively on scholarship and training in

European art music, but over time some have expanded their purview to include jazz, popular music, music technology, and a few courses in world music. Even in this otherwise welcoming context, ethnomusicologists have struggled with an entrenched value system predicated on the unexamined judgment that European art music is better and more worthy of study than other kinds of music, and that the musicians and people who make, support, and study European art music are superior to those making, supporting, and studying other kinds of music. In music schools, ethnomusicologists are expected to teach principally about world music in courses with titles like "music cultures of the world," a practice that reinforces a limited view of the "study-objects" of ethnomusicology. In this environment, their greatest contribution may be the conveyance of values and attitudes that they hope will counter the exclusionary aesthetics and ethics of most music schools and departments. As Ellen Koskoff puts it, ethnomusicologists teach a "bedrock philosophy" that "all people and all musics . . . have equivalent meaning [and value] to someone, somewhere." They teach students "to become good musical citizens in [the] world," and they ask them to learn "open-mindedness, fairness and compassion for differences of all kinds."

In some cases, because the courses ethnomusicologists teach tend be quite popular, some music schools and departments have added a second, third, and even more ethnomusicologists, giving them a critical mass to form a doctoral program in the field at the school. Today, there are more than twenty doctoral programs in ethnomusicology in American universities, and between ten and twenty programs in Great Britain and Ireland. Even in universities where ethnomusicological study flourishes at the graduate level, ethnomusicologists still have to fight an uphill battle to expose undergraduate music majors to a global perspective on the broad range of music they will surely encounter during their musical careers and to introduce them to an egalitarian and worldly system of values.

The public and private sectors

In addition to university teaching, ethnomusicologists today work in many other institutional settings, including K-12 schools; research institutions such as archives, libraries, and museums; governmental and public institutions such as (in the United States) the National Endowment for the Arts, the National Endowment for the Humanities, the Library of Congress, the Smithsonian Institution, public broadcasting, state and local folk arts agencies, and religious institutions. Even the music, film, and television industries find ethnomusicologists useful, especially in the areas of intellectual property rights, licensing, and research.

Some ethnomusicologists have made a career in K-12 music teaching or in the training of such teachers at the university level. Among the ethnomusicological themes Patricia Campbell has identified as particularly fruitful for music educators are cross-cultural perspectives on music cognition; mind-body and music-dance dualities; children's music culture; pedagogy of world music; and research approaches to the study of musical thought and musical behavior.

Ethnomusicologists have often been called upon to provide leadership in governmental and public institutions, including, in the United States, Bill Ivey, former chair from 1998 to 2001 of the National Endowment for the Arts (NEA); William Ferris, chairman of the National Endowment for the Humanities (NEH) from 1997 to 2001; Bess Lomax Hawes and Daniel Sheehy, heads of the Folk Arts Program of the NEA; and Robert Garfias, presidential appointee to the National Council on the Arts. Ethnomusicologists sit on the Board of Trustees and the staff of the American Folklife Center at the Library of Congress, an important repository of America's musical heritage. In 1987 the Smithsonian Institution acquired Folkways Records, which had made pioneering recordings not only of American folk and blues musicians but also of world music. The ethnomusicologist

Anthony Seeger was its first director from 1988 to 2000, and he and his successors have turned it into one of the leading producers of recordings of music from all over the world, recordings graced by extensive and authoritative notes. They also pioneered the payment of fees and royalties to traditional artists, many of whom had been denied appropriate remuneration in years past.

Sound archives have been particularly important institutions for ethnomusicological work. From the earliest days of phonograph recordings to the present, ethnomusicologists have deposited their field recordings in archives, and some have made careers working in them. The earliest were the Vienna Phonogrammarchiv, founded in 1899, and the Berliner Phonogramm-Archiv, directed by Erich von Hornbostel from 1905 to 1933. Today, large international collections are held at the British Library Sound Archive, the American Folklife Center at the Library of Congress, and the Indiana University Archives of Traditional Music. Other national archives, such as the Archive and Research Center for Ethnomusicology in India, the National Film and Sound Archive in Australia, and the Canadian Museum of Civilization Archives, play important roles in preserving a record of local musical traditions.

The ethnomusicologists who work in sound archives, whether large international ones or small local ones, face a plethora of ethical issues. For example, the descendents of people whose songs were recorded and deposited decades earlier may question whether and how they should be distributed to the public. Or they may ask for the recordings to be repatriated to the communities in which they were made or to the families of those who recorded them.

Ethnomusicologists are often called upon to curate, produce, and create concerts and festivals that showcase musicians whom they champion or who represent musical cultures they have studied. The Smithsonian Folklife Festival, held annually on the Mall in Washington, DC, is only one of hundreds of similar festivals that ethnomusicologists facilitate and manage for the benefit of the artists, the public-policy agendas of the sponsors, and the general public.

A few ethnomusicologists have found work in the commercial music and film industries, often researching, selecting, and licensing music for online encyclopedias, film scores, and games. In an unusual recent example the ethnomusicologist Wanda Bryant assisted the writer and director James Cameron and the composer James Horner in the creation of a new "music culture" for the Na'vi people of the planet Pandora in the 2009 3-D blockbuster film *Avatar*. Bryant gathered hundreds of recordings from around the world for the composer to review; hired Los Angeles–area singers from many "ethnic" traditions to record songs in the newly created Na'vi language; and imagined a Na'vi culture requiring musical genres such as Hunt Song, Funeral Lament, and Weaving Song. Horner took these elements, mashed

10. Ethnomusicologist Daniel Sheehy interviews Colombian *guacharaca* (rasp) player Jaime Maestre as part of a comparative workshop on Latin American percussion instruments at the 2009 Smithsonian Folklife Festival on the National Mall in Washington, DC.

them up into largely unrecognizable synthesized combinations, and included them in a traditional Hollywood orchestral score.

Public service

Ethnomusicologists, by nature, are given to public service in one form or another. For starters, they want to reciprocate the hospitality and cooperation they receive from their consultants in the field. Often they help the musicians they befriend by producing a recording, writing "record jacket" notes, organizing concerts, and helping spread the word about musical traditions they believe deserve wider recognition. Sometimes they help them gain fame and a bit of fortune by facilitating, or translating for, a world tour. This impulse has been translated by a few into either a career dedicated to public service or to an "applied ethnomusicology" dedicated to improving the quality of intergroup relations in fraught circumstances; helping to sustain endangered musical cultures; or aiding social groups and musicians intent on improving their lot in the world. Svanibor Pettan from Croatia and Slovenia, Samuel Araujo from Brazil, Ursula Hemetek from Austria, and Bess Lomax Hawes, Daniel Sheehy, and Anthony Seeger from the United States have been among the leaders in this area. In Germany Britta Sweers, in the wake of an outbreak of violence by Neo-Nazi skinheads against immigrant Roma from Romania and Vietnamese guest workers, helped to produce a CD of music to teach schoolchildren about interethnic tolerance and the "polyphony of cultures." Katherine Van Buren, Gregory Barz and others are studying the role of music in educating people about the scourge of HIV/AIDS. They help local activists and organizers in many parts of the world, but especially in Africa, to use music in their grassroots missions to solve intractable health problems at the same time that they document their activities and evaluate the effectiveness of their musical interventions.

Twenty years ago there was some tension between supposedly pure, theoretical work and public-sector, applied, or practical work. Today, as more and more ethnomusicologists engage with people and communities enduring serious social, medical, and political problems, this dichotomy is fast disappearing in favor of what Anthony Seeger has called "theories forged in the crucible of action."

Ethnomusicologists are increasingly asking themselves the question, "Ethnomusicology for what purpose?" There are many possible answers to this question. In the academy, for example, ethnomusicologists are telling stories about human music making and its significance in all places and times, stories that challenge other stories based on extremely limited, deeply entrenched, and uncritically received and proclaimed Eurocentric notions about musical values and repertoires. Ethnomusicologists' stories broaden and enrich students' understanding of the nature of music, and in some cases have a direct impact on their musical practice.

Outside the university, especially when ethnomusicologists work in places troubled by war, violence, social inequality, or epidemic disease, they try to make their work relevant and useful to those they study, in some cases improving the quality of people's lives. As John Blacking eloquently put it:

> Ethnomusicology can be influential in the world if it can help to find ways of using the performing arts to enlighten the materially powerful, increase the power of the politically weak, enrich the emotional experience of all, and ensure the maintenance of the peaceful, co-operative relationships that make for good living as much as successful musical performance.

Ethnomusicologists today are fully engaged with the world of music as they find it, not as some might wish it to be. Although an older generation began its work with a deep and abiding appreciation of the value of traditional music and often ignored newer forms of music that were responding to new political and social realities, today's ethnomusicologists study and write about popular and emerging forms of music the world over, as well as about the uses to which musicians, listeners, producers, and governmental, religious, and private institutions put them.

The study of traditional music taught ethnomusicologists about the important functions of music in human psychological and social life. The understandings of the nature of music they gained in those studies have prepared the field well for interpreting how the modern and postmodern explosion of new forms of music around the world is serving individuals on the move as well as rapidly changing, dissolving, and reforming societies dealing with the enormous psychological, social, political, and economic problems of the modern world. Rather than facing that predicted musical "gray-out," ethnomusicologists are struggling to keep abreast of old, new, and emerging music scenes and genres that speak to humankind's enduring attempt to understand and tell stories about itself by making music and being musical. In other words, ethnomusicologists will always have plenty of work to do.

References

Chapter 1

John Blacking, *How Musical Is Man?* (Seattle: University of Washington Press, 1973), quote from 116.

Jaap Kunst, *Ethnomusicology*, 3rd ed. (The Hague: M. Nijhoff, 1959), quote from 1.

Alan Merriam, "Ethnomusicology: Discussion and Definition of the Field," *Ethnomusicology* 4 (1960):107–14, quotes from 109.

Mark Slobin, *Subcultural Sounds: Micromusics of the West* (Hanover, NH: Wesleyan University Press, 1993).

Christopher Small, *Musicking: The Meanings of Performing and Listening* (Hanover, NH: Wesleyan University Press, 1998).

Jeff Todd Titon et al., *Worlds of Music*, 2nd ed. (New York: Schirmer Books, 1992).

Chapter 2

Guido Adler, "The Scope, Method, and Aim of Musicology," trans. and with commentary by Erica Mugglestone, *Yearbook for Traditional Music* 13 (1981 [1885]): 1–21.

Judith Becker, *Deep Listeners: Music, Emotion, and Trancing* (Bloomington: Indiana University Press, 2004).

Charles Burney, *The Present State of Music in France and Italy* (London, 1771).

Alexander John Ellis, "On the Musical Scales of Various Nations," *Journal of the Society of Arts* 33 (1885): 485–527, quote from 526.

Kenneth J. DeWoskin, *A Song for One or Two: Music and the Concept of Art in Early China* (Ann Arbor: University of Michigan Center for Chinese Studies, 1982).
Nicholas M. England et al., "Symposium on Transcription and Analysis: A Hukwe Song with Musical Bow," *Ethnomusicology* 8, no. 3 (1964): 223–77.
Mantle Hood, *The Ethnomusicologist* (New York: McGraw-Hill, 1971).
Sir William Jones, "On the Musical Scales of the Hindoos," *Asiatick Researches* 3 (1792): 55–87.
Mieczyslaw Kolinski, "Classification of Tonal Structures," *Studies in Ethnomusicology* 1 (1961): 38–76.
Assen D. Kresteff, "Music Disciplina and Musica Sonora," *Journal of Research in Music Education* 10, no. 1 (1962): 13–29.
René T. A. Lysloff and Leslie C. Gay Jr., eds., *Music and Technoculture* (Middletown, CT: Wesleyan University Press, 2003).
Alan P. Merriam, *The Anthropology of Music* (Evanston, IL: Northwestern University Press, 1964), quotes from 32.
Bruno Nettl, *North American Indian Musical Styles* (Philadelphia: American Folklore Society, 1954).
J. H. Kwabena Nketia, "The Problem of Meaning in African Music," *Ethnomusicology* 6, no. 1 (1962): 1–7.
Lewis Rowell, *Music and Musical Thought in Early India* (Chicago: University of Chicago Press, 1992).
George Sawa, *Music Performance Practice in the Early 'Abbasid Era 132–320 AH/750–932 AD.* (Toronto: Pontifical Institute of Mediaeval Studies, 1989).
Jonathan Sterne, "Sounds Like the Mall of America: Programmed Music and the Architectonics of Commercial Space," *Ethnomusicology* 41, no. 1 (1997): 22–50.
Robert M. Stevenson, *Music in Aztec and Inca Territory* (Berkeley: University of California Press, 1968).
Carl Stumpf, "Lieder der Bellakula-Indianer," *Vierteljahrschrift für Musikwissenchaft* 2 (1886): 405–26.
Erich M. von Hornbostel and Curt Sachs, "Systematik der Musikinstrumente: ein Versuch," *Zeitshrift für Ethnologie* 46 (1914): 553–90; Eng. trans. in *Galpin Society Journal* 14 (1961): 3–29.
Christopher Waterman, "*Jùjú* History: Toward a Theory of Sociomusical Practice," in *Ethnomusicology and Modern Music History*, ed. Stephen Blum et al. (Urbana: University of Illinois Press, 1990), 49–67, quote from 66.
M. I. West, *Ancient Greek Music* (Oxford: Clarendon Press, 1992).

Chapter 3

Simha Arom, *African Polyphony and Polyrhythm: Musical Structure and Methodology* (Cambridge: Cambridge University Press, 1991).

Gregory F. Barz, "Confronting the Field(Note) In and Out of the Field: Music, Voices, Text, and Experience in Dialogue," in *Shadows in the Field: New Perspectives for Fieldwork in Ethnomusicology*, ed. Gregory F. Barz and Timothy J. Cooley, 2nd ed. (New York: Oxford University Press, 1997), 45–62.

Paul Berliner, *The Soul of Mbira: Music and Traditions of the Shona People of Zimbabwe* (Berkeley: University of California Press, 1978).

Peter Crossley-Holland, ed., *The Melograph*, special issue of *Selected Reports in Ethnomusicology* 2, no. 1 (Los Angeles: UCLA Ethnomusicology Publications, 1974).

Beverley Diamond and Pirkko Moisala, "Music and Gender: Negotiating Shifting Worlds," in *Music and Gender*, ed. Pirkko Moisala and Beverley Diamond (Urbana: University of Illinois Press, 2000), 1–23.

Mantle Hood, "The Challenge of Bi-Musicality," *Ethnomusicology* 4, no. 1 (1960): 55–59.

Frank Mitchell, *Blessingway Singer: The Autobiography of Frank Mitchell, 1881–1967*, ed. Charlotte Frisbie and David McAllester (Tucson: University of Arizona Press, 1978).

Regula Burckhardt Qureshi, *Sufi Music of India and Pakistan: Sound, Context and Meaning in Qawwali* (Chicago: University of Chicago Press, 1995 [1986]), quote from 143.

Timothy Rice, "Understanding and Producing the Variability of Oral Tradition: Learning from a Bulgarian Bagpiper," *Journal of American Folklore* 108, no. 429 (1995): 266–76.

Hiromi Lorraine Sakata, *Afghanistan Encounters with Music and Friends* (Costa Mesa, CA: Mazda Publishers, 2013).

Anthony Seeger, "Ethnomusicologists, Archives, Professional Organizations, and the Shifting Ethics of Intellectual Property," *Yearbook for Traditional Music* 28 (1996): 87–105; quote from 90.

Kay Kaufman Shelemay, *A Song of Longing: An Ethiopian Journey* (Urbana: University of Illinois Press, 1991).

Jeff Todd Titon, "Music, the Public Interest, and the Practice of Ethnomusicology," *Ethnomusicology* 36, no. 3 (1992): 315–22; quote from 321.

Hugo Zemp, "'Are'are Classification of Musical Types and Instruments." *Ethnomusicology* 22, no. 1 (1978): 37–67.

Hugo Zemp, "Aspects of 'Are'Are Musical Theory," *Ethnomusicology* 23, no. 1 (1979): 5–48.

Hugo Zemp, "The/An Ethnomusicologist and the Record Business," *Yearbook for Traditional Music* 28 (1996): 36–55.

Chapter 4

Judith Becker and Alton Becker, "A Musical Icon: Power and Meaning in Javanese Gamelan Music," in *The Sign in Music and Literature*, ed. Wendy Steiner (Austin: University of Texas Press, 1981), 203–15.

Pierre Bourdieu, *Outline of a Theory of Practice* (Cambridge: Cambridge University Press, 1977).

Maya Deren, *Divine Horsemen: The Living Gods of Haiti* (London: Thames and Hudson, 1984).

Clifford Geertz, *Interpretation of Cultures: Selected Essays* (New York: Basic Books, 1973).

Henry Kingsbury, *Music, Talent, and Performance: A Conservatory Cultural System* (Philadelphia: Temple University Press, 1988), quotes from 122, 123, 126.

Claude Lévi-Strauss, *Structural Anthropology* (New York: Basic Books, 1963).

Alan Lomax, *Folk Song Style and Culture* (Washington, DC: American Association for the Advancement of Science, 1968), quote from 133.

Alan Lomax, *Cantometrics* (Berkeley: University of California Extension Media Center, 1976), quotes from 13, 17.

David McAllester, "Reminiscences of the Early Days," *Ethnomusicology* 50, no. 2 (2006): 199–203.

Alan P. Merriam, "Uses and Function," in *The Anthropology of Music* (Evanston, IL: Northwestern University Press, 1964), 209–28.

Daniel M. Neuman, *The Life of Music in North India: The Organization of an Artistic Tradition* (Detroit: Wayne State University Press, 1980).

Timothy Rice, "Bulgaria or Chalgaria: The Attenuation of Bulgarian Nationalism in a Mass-Mediated Popular Music," *Yearbook for Traditional Music* 34 (2002): 25–46.

Timothy Rice, "Time, Place, and Metaphor in Musical Experience and Ethnography," *Ethnomusicology* 47, no. 2 (2003): 151–79.

Anthony Seeger, *Why Suyá Sing: A Musical Anthropology of an Amazonian People* (Urbana: University of Illinois Press, 2004 [1987]), quote from 78.

Michael Tenzer, ed., *Analytical Studies in World Music* (New York: Oxford University Press, 2006), quote from 4.
Michael Tenzer, "Generalized Representations of Musical Time and Periodic Structures, *Ethnomusicology* 55, no. 3 (2011): 369–86.
Thomas Turino, *Moving Away from Silence: Music of the Peruvian Altiplano and the Experience of Urban Migration* (Chicago: University of Chicago Press, 1993), quote from 77.
Thomas Turino, *Music as Social Life: The Politics of Participation* (Chicago: University of Chicago Press, 2008), quotes from 1, 5–16.
Thomas Turino, "Signs of Imagination, Identity, and Experience: A Peircean Semiotic Theory for Music," *Ethnomusicology* 43, no. 2 (1999): 221–55, quotes from 224, 250.
Colin M. Turnbull, *The Forest People* (New York: Simon and Schuster, 1961).
Christopher A. Waterman, "'I'm a Leader, Not a Boss': Social Identity and Popular Music in Ibadan, Nigeria," *Ethnomusicology* 26, no. 1 (1982): 59–71; quotes from 67, 68.
Richard A. Waterman, "Music in Aboriginal Culture—Some Sociological and Psychological Implications" (1956); quoted in Merriam, *Anthropology of Music*, 225.
Leslie A. White, *The Pueblo of Sia, New Mexico* (1962); quoted in Merriam, *Anthropology of Music*, 225.

Chapter 5

Judith Becker, *Deep Listeners: Music, Emotion, and Trancing* (Bloomington: Indiana University Press, 2004), quote from 29.
Paul F. Berliner, *The Soul of Mbira: Music and Traditions of the Shona People of Zimbabwe* (Chicago: University of Chicago Press, 1991 [1978]).
Paul F. Berliner, *Thinking in Jazz: The Infinite Art of Improvisation* (Chicago: University of Chicago Press, 1994), quotes from 31–33.
John Blacking, *Music, Culture, and Experience: Selected Papers of John Blacking*, ed. Reginald Byron (Chicago: University of Chicago Press, 1995).
Steven Feld, "'Flow Like a Waterfall': The Metaphors of Kaluli Music Theory," *Yearbook for Traditional Music* 13 (1981): 22–47; quote from 30.
Steven Friedson, *Dancing Prophets: Musical Experience in Tumbuka Healing* (Chicago: University of Chicago Press, 1996), quotes from 100, 143, 161–62.

Chris Goertzen, "Powwows and Identity on the Piedmont and Coastal Plains of North Carolina," *Ethnomusicology* 45, no. 1 (2001): 58–88; quotes from 68, 71.

Ellen Koskoff, "An Introduction to Women, Music, and Culture," in *Women and Music in Cross-Cultural Perspective*, ed. Ellen Koskoff (Urbana: University of Illinois Press, 1987), 1–23.

Peter Manuel, "Puerto Rican Music and Cultural Identity: Creative Appropriation of Cuban Sources from Danza to Salsa," *Ethnomusicology* 38 (1994): 249–80.

Alan P. Merriam, *The Anthropology of Music* (Evanston, IL: Northwestern University Press, 1964).

Alan P. Merriam, *The Ethnomusicology of the Flathead Indians* (New York: Wenner-Gren Foundation, 1967).

Andrew Neher, "A Physiological Explanation of Unusual Ceremonies Involving Drums," *Human Biology* 4 (1962): 151–60.

Gilbert Rouget, *Music and Trance: A Theory of the Relations between Music and Possession* (Chicago: University of Chicago Press, 1985), quote from 323.

Anthony Seeger, *Why Suyá Sing: A Musical Anthropology of an Amazonian People* (Cambridge: Cambridge University Press, 1987), quotes from 53–54.

Martin Stokes, "Introduction: Ethnicity, Identity and Music," in *Ethnicity, Identity and Music: The Musical Construction of Place*, ed. Martin Stokes (New York: Berg, 1994), 1–27.

Jane C. Sugarman, *Engendering Song: Singing and Subjectivity at Prespa Albanian Weddings* (Chicago: University of Chicago Press, 1997), quotes from 201, 235, 251.

Christopher A. Waterman, "'Our Tradition Is a Very Modern Tradition': Popular Music and the Construction of Pan-Yoruba Identity," *Ethnomusicology* 34, no. 3 (1990): 367–79; quote from 375–76.

Chapter 6

Harris M. Berger, *Metal, Rock and Jazz: Perception and the Phenomenology of Musical Experience* (Middletown, CT: Wesleyan University Press, 1999).

Benjamin Brinner, *Knowing Music, Making Music: Javanese Gamelan and the Theory of Musical Competence and Interaction* (Chicago: University of Chicago Press).

Virginia Danielson, *The Voice of Egypt: Umm Kulthūm, Arabic Song, and Egyptian Society in the Twentieth Century* (Chicago: University of Chicago Press, 1997).
Catherine J. Hagedorn, *Divine Utterances: The Performance of Afro-Cuban Santería* (Washington, DC: Smithsonian Institution Press, 2001).
Steven Loza, *Tito Puente and the Making of Latin Music* (Urbana: University of Illinois Press, 1999).
Bruno Nettl, "In Honor of Our Principal Teachers," *Ethnomusicology* 28, no. 2 (1984): 173–85.
Manuel H. Peña, *The Texas-Mexican Conjunto: History of a Working-Class Music* (Austin: University of Texas Press, 1985).
Timothy Rice, *May It Fill Your Soul: Experiencing Bulgarian Music* (Chicago: University of Chicago Press, 1994).
Raúl R. Romero, *Debating the Past: Music, Memory, and Identity in the Andes* (New York: Oxford University Press, 2001).
Jesse D. Ruskin and Timothy Rice, "The Individual in Musical Ethnography," *Ethnomusicology* 56, no. 2 (2012): 299–327.
Michael Veal, *Fela: The Life and Times of an African Musical Icon* (Philadelphia: Temple University Press, 2000).
Lise A. Waxer, *The City of Musical Memory: Salsa, Record Grooves, and Popular Culture in Cali, Columbia* (Middletown, CT: Wesleyan University Press, 2002), quotes from 134, 138.

Chapter 7

Judith O. Becker, *Traditional Music in Modern Java* (Honolulu: University of Hawaii Press, 1980).
Stephen Blum, Philip V. Bohlman, and Daniel M. Neuman, eds., *Ethnomusicological and Modern Music History* (Urbana: University of Illinois Press, 1991).
Philip V. Bohlman, "Of *Yekkes* and Chamber Music in Israel: Ethnomusicological Meaning in European Music History, " in *Ethnomusicology and Modern Music History*, ed. Stephen Blum et al., 254–67 (Urbana: University of Illinois Press, 1991), quotes from 261, 266, 267.
David Coplan, "Ethnomusicology and the Meaning of Tradition," in Blum et al., *Ethnomusicological and Modern Music History*, 35–48, quote from 35.
Joseph S. C. Lam, *State Sacrifices and Music in Ming China: Orthodoxy, Creativity, and Expressiveness* (Albany: State University of New York Press, 1998), quote from xii.

Peter Manuel, *Cassette Culture: Popular Music and Technology in North India* (Chicago: University of Chicago Press, 1993).

Bruno Nettl, *The Study of Ethnomusicology: Twenty-nine Issues and Concepts* (Urbana: University of Illinois Press, 1983), quotes from 11.

A.J. Racy, "Historical Worldviews of Early Ethnomusicologists: An East-West Encounter in Cairo, 1932," in Blum et al., 68–91, *Ethnomusicology and Modern Music History*, quotes from 74, 88.

Ljerka V. Rasmussen, *Newly Composed Folk Music of Yugoslavia* (New York: Routledge, 2002).

George Sawa, *Music Performance Practice in the Early 'Abbasid Era. 750–932 A.D.* (Toronto: Pontifical Institute of Medieval Studies, 2004 [1989]).

Kay Kaufman Shelemay, "'Historical Ethnomusicology': Reconstructing Falasha Liturgical History," *Ethnomusicology* 24, no. 2 (1980): 233–58.

Richard A. Waterman, "African Influences on American Negro Music," in *Acculturation in the Americas*, ed. Sol Tax, 227–44 (Chicago: University of Chicago Press, 1952).

Chapter 8

Michael Bakan et al., "Following Frank: Response-Ability and the Co-creation of Culture in a Medical Ethnomusicology Program for Children on the Autism Spectrum," *Ethnomusicology* 52, no. 2 (2008): 163–202.

Gregory Barz, *Singing for Life: HIV/AIDS and Music in Uganda* (New York: Routledge, 2006).

Emma Baulch, *Making Scenes: Reggae, Punk, and Death Metal in 1990s Bali* (Durham, NC: Duke University Press, 2007).

William Cheng, "Role-playing toward a Virtual Musical Democracy in *The Lord of the Rings Online*," *Ethnomuusicology* 56, no. 1 (2012): 31–62, quotes from 57, 58.

David Cooper, "Fife and Fiddle: Protestants and Traditional Music in Northern Ireland," in *Music and Conflict*, ed. John Morgan O'Connell and Salwa El-Shawan Castelo-Branco, 89–106 (Urbana: University of Illinois Press, 2010).

Suzanne G. Cusick, "Music as Torture/Music as Weapon," *TRANS-Transcultural Music Review* 10, article 11, (2006). Accessed August 18, 2012.

Keila Diehl, *Echoes from Dharamsala: Music in the Life of a Tibetan Refugee Community* (Berkeley: University of California Press, 2002).
Veronica Doubleday, "9/11 and the Politics of Music-Making in Afghanistan," in *Music in the Post-9/11 World*, ed. Jonathan Ritter and J. Martin Daughtry, 277–314 (New York: Routledge, 2007), quote from 309.
Steven Feld, "Notes on World Beat," *Public Culture* 1, no. 1 (1988): 31–17; quotes on 31, 34.
Steven Feld, "A Sweet Lullaby for World Music," *Public Culture* 12, no. 1 (2000): 145–71; quote on 146.
Steven Feld, "Waterfalls of Song: An Acoustemology of Place Resounding in Bosavi, Papua New Guinea," in *Senses of Place*, ed. Steven Feld and Keith H. Basso, 91–135 (Santa Fe, NM: School of American Research Press, 1996).
Nancy Guy, "Flowing Down Taiwan's Tamsui River: Towards an Ecomusicology of the Environmental Imagination," *Ethnomusicology* 53, no. 2 (2009): 218–48.
Huang Hao, "*Yaogun Yinyue:* Rethinking Mainland Chinese Rock 'n' roll," *Popular Music* 20, no. 1 (2001): 1–11.
Keith Kahn-Harris, "'Roots'?: The Relationship between the Global and the Local in the Extreme Metal Scene," *Popular Music* 19, no. 1 (2000): 13–28.
Ward Keeler, "What's Burmese about Burmese Rap? Why Some Expressive Forms Go Global," *American Ethnologist* 36, no. 1 (2009): 2–19.
Charles Keil, "Music Mediated and Live in Japan," *Ethnomusicology* 28, no. 1 (1984): 91–96, quote from 94.
Benjamin D. Koen, "Music-Prayer-Meditation Dynamics in Healing," in *The Oxford Handbook of Medical Ethnomusicology*, ed. Benjamin Koen et al., 93–119 (New York: Oxford University Press, 2008).
René T. A. Lysloff, "Mozart in Mirrorshades: Ethnomusicology, Technology, and the Politics of Representation," *Ethnomusicology* 41, no. 2 (1997): 206–19, quote from 215.
René T. A. Lysloff and Leslie C. Gay Jr., eds., *Music and Technoculture* (Middletown, CT: Wesleyan University Press, 2003), quote from 2.
Louise Meintjes, "Paul Simon's *Graceland*, South Africa, and the Mediation of Musical Meaning," *Ethnomusicology* 34, no. 1 (1990): 37–73.
Louise Meintjes, *Sound of Africa! Making Music Zulu in a South African Studio* (Durham, NC: Duke University Press, 2003), quotes from 7, 8.

John Morgan O'Connell and Salwa El-Shawan Castelo-Branco, eds., *Music and Conflict* (Urbana: University of Illinois Press, 2010), quotes from 7, 243.

Svanibor Pettan, ed., *Music, Politics, and War: Views from Croatia* (Zagreb: Institute of Ethnology and Folklore Research, 1998).

David B. Pruett, "When the Tribe Goes Platinum: A Case Study toward an Ethnomusicology of Mainstream Popular Music in the U.S.," *Ethnomusicology* 55, no. 1 (2011): 1–30.

Tina K. Ramnarine, "Acoustemology, Indigeneity, and Joik in Valkeapää's Symphonic Activism: Views from Europe's Arctic Fringes for Environmental Ethnomusicology," *Ethnomusicology* 53, no. 2 (2009): 187–217; quotes from 203, 205, 209–10.

Jonathan Ritter and J. Martin Daughtry, eds., *Music in the Post-9/11 World* (New York: Routledge, 2007).

R. Murray Schafer, *The Tuning of the World* (New York: Knopf, 1977).

Anthony Seeger, "The Suya and the White Man: Forty-five years of Musical Diplomacy in Brazil," in *Music and Conflict*, ed. John Morgan O'Connell and Salwa El-Shawan Castelo-Branco, 109–25 (Urbana: University of Illinois Press, 2010), quote from 113.

Thomas Solomon, "'Living Underground Is Tough': Authenticity and Locality in the Hip-hop Community in Istanbul, Turkey," *Popular Music* 24, no. 1 (2005): 1–20.

Timothy D. Taylor, *Global Pop: World Music, World Markets* (New York: Routledge, 1997), quotes from 149, 157.

Chapter 9

Patricia S. Campbell, "Ethnomusicology and Music Education: Crossroads for Knowing Music, Education, and Culture," *Research Studies in Music Education* 21 (2003):16–30.

Ellen Koskoff, "What Do We Want to Teach Them When We Teach Music? One Apology, Two Short Ripostes, Three Ethical Dilemmas, and Eighty-two Questions," in *Rethinking Music*, ed. Nicholas Cook and Mark Everist (Oxford: Oxford University Press, 1999), quote from 558–59.

Sylvia Nannyonga-Tamusuza and Andrew N. Weintraub, "The Audible Future: Reimagining the Role of Sound Archives and Sound Repatriation in Uganda," *Ethnomusicology* 56, no. 2 (2012): 206–33.

Helen Rees, "The Dongjing Music Revival: Have Music, Will Travel," in *Echoes of History: Naxi Music in Modern China* (New York: Oxford University Press, 2000).

Victoria Rogers, "John Blacking: Social and Political Activist," *Ethnomusicology* 56, no. 1 (2012): 63–85, quote from 80.
Anthony Seeger, "Theories Forged in the Crucible of Action," in *Shadows in the Field: New Perspectives for Fieldwork in Ethnomusicology*, ed. Gregory Barz and Timothy J. Cooley, 271–88, 2nd ed. (New York: Oxford University Press, 2008).
Martin Stokes, "Introduction: Ethnicity, Identity and Music," in *Ethnicity, Identity, and Music: The Musical Construction of Place*, ed. Martin Stokes, 1–27 (New York: Berg, 1994), quote from 1.
Britta Sweers, "Polyphony of Cultures: Conceptualization and Consequences of an Applied Media Project," in *Applied Ethnomusicology: Historical and Contemporary Approaches*, ed. Klisala Harrison et al., 214–32 (Newcastle upon Tyne, UK: Cambridge Scholars, 2010).
Katherine J. Van Buren, "Applied Ethnomusicology and HIV and AIDS: Responsibility, Ability, and Action," *Ethnomusicology* 54, no. 2 (2010): 202–23.

Further reading

Chapter 2

Askew, Kelly. *Performing the Nation: Swahili Music and Cultural Politics in Tanzania*. Chicago: University of Chicago Press, 2002.

Bendix, Regina. *In Search of Authenticity: The Formation of Folklore Studies*. Madison: University of Wisconsin Press, 1997.

Bohlman, Philip. *Focus: Music, Nationalism, and the Making of the New Europe*. New York: Routledge, 2011.

Browner, Tara. *Heartbeat of the People: Music and Dance of the Northern Pow-wow*. Urbana: University of Illinois Press, 2002.

McAllester, David P. *Enemy Way Music*. Cambridge, MA: The Peabody Museum, 1954.

McLean, Mervyn. *Pioneers of Ethnomusicology*. Coral Springs, FL: Llumina Press, 2006.

Myers, Helen, ed. *Ethnomusicology: Historical and Regional Studies*. New York: W. W. Norton, 1993.

Nettl, Bruno. *Nettl's Elephant: On the History of Ethnomusicology*. Urbana: University of Illinois Press, 2008.

Nettl, Bruno. *The Study of Ethnomusicology: Thirty-one Issues and Concepts*. Urbana: University of Illinois Press, 2005.

Nettl, Bruno, and Philip V. Bohlman, eds., *Comparative Musicology and Anthropology of Music*. Chicago: University of Chicago Press, 1991.

Nketia, J. H. Kwabena. *African Music in Ghana*. Evanston, IL: Northwestern University Press, 1963.

Post, Jennifer C. *Ethnomusicology: A Research and Information Guide.* New York: Routledge, 2011.

Sachs, Curt. *The History of Musical Instruments.* New York: W. W. Norton, 1940.

Seeger, Charles. *Studies in Musicology.* Berkeley: University of California Press, 1977.

Stumpf, Carl. *Die Anfänge der Musik.* Leipzig: J. A. Barth, 1911.

Stobart, Henry, ed. *The New (Ethno)musicologies.* Lanham, MD: Scarecrow Press, 2008.

Stone, Ruth et al., eds. *Garland Encyclopedia of World Music.* New York: Routledge, 1998–2002.

von Hornbostel, Erich M. "Melodie und Skala." *Jahrbuch der Musikbibliothek Peters* 19 (1913): 11–23.

Wallaschek, Richard. *Primitive Music: An Inquiry into the Origin and Development of Music, Songs, Instruments, Dances and Pantomimes of Savage Races.* London, 1893. Reprint, New York: Da Capo, 1940.

Witzleben, J. Lawrence. "Whose Ethnomusicology? European Ethnomusicology and the Study of Asian Music." *Ethnomusicology* 41, no. 2 (1997): 220–42.

Wong, Deborah. *Speak It Louder: Asian Americans Making Music.* New York: Routledge, 2004.

Chapter 3

Barz, Gregory, and Timothy J. Cooley, eds. *Shadows in the Field: New Perspectives on Fieldwork in Ethnomusicology*, 2nd ed. New York: Oxford University Press, 2008.

Blum, Stephen. "Analysis of Musical Style." In Myers, *Ethnomusicology: An Introduction*, 165–218.

Ellingson, Ter. "Transcription." In Myers, *Ethnomusicology: An Introduction*, 110–52.

Guy, Nancy. "Trafficking in Taiwan Aboriginal Voices." In *Handle With Care: Ownership and Control of Ethnographic Materials*, edited by Sjoerd R. Jaarsma, 195–209. Pittsburgh: University of Pittsburgh Press, 2002.

Headland, Thomas N., Kenneth L. Pike, and Marvin Harris. *Emics and Etics: the Insider/Outsider Debate.* Newbury Park, CA: Sage, 1990.

Myers, Helen, ed. *Ethnomusicology: An Introduction.* New York: W. W. Norton, 1992.

Myers, Helen. "Fieldwork." In Myers, *Ethnomusicology: An Introduction*, 21–49.
Mills, Sherylle. "Indigenous Music and the Law: An Analysis of National and International Legislation." *Yearbook for Traditional Music* 28 (1996): 57–86.
Rees, Helen. "The Age of Consent: Traditional Music, Intellectual Property, and Changing Attitudes in the People's Republic of China." *British Journal of Ethnomusicology* 12, no. 1 (2003): 137–71.
Seeger, Anthony. "Ethnography of Music." In Myers, *Ethnomusicology: An Introduction*, 88–109.
Solís, Ted, ed., *Performing Ethnomusicology: Teaching and Representation in World Music Ensembles*. Berkeley: University of California Press, 2004.
Weintraub, Andrew, and Bell Yung, eds. *Music and Cultural Rights*. Evanston: University of Illinois Press, 2009.

Chapter 4

Berger, Harris M. *Stance: Ideas about Emotion, Style, and Meaning for the Study of Expressive Culture*. Middletown, CT: Wesleyan University Press, 2009.
Nattiez, Jean-Jacques. *Music and Discourse: Toward a Semiology of Music*. Princeton, NJ: Princeton University Press, 1990.
Stone, Ruth. *Theory for Ethnomusicology*. Upper Saddle River, NJ: Pearson Prentice Hall, 2008.

Chapter 5

Clayton, Martin, Trevor Herbert, and Richard Middleton, eds. *The Cultural Study of Music: A Critical Introduction*. New York: Routledge, 2003.
Jankowski, Richard C. *Stambeli: Music, Trance, and Alterity in Tunisia*. Chicago: University of Chicago Press, 2010.
Norton, Barley. *Songs for the Spirits: Music and Mediums in Modern Vietnam*. Urbana: University of Illinois Press, 2009.
Radano, Ronald, and Philip V. Bohlman, eds. *Music and the Racial Imagination*. Chicago: University of Chicago Press, 2000.
Racy, A. J. *Making Music in the Arab World*. Cambridge: Cambridge University Press, 2003.

Roseman, Marina. *Healing Sounds from the Malaysian Rainforest: Temiar Music and Medicine*. Berkeley: University of California Press, 1991.

Chapter 6

Garcia, David F. *Arsenio Rodriguez and the Transnational Flows of Latin Popular Music*. Philadelphia: Temple University Press, 2006.

Jones, Stephen. *Plucking the Winds: Lives of Village Musicians in Old and New China*. Leiden: CHIME Foundation, 2004.

Porter, James. *Jeannie Robertson: Emergent Singer, Transformative Voice*. Knoxville: University of Tennessee Press, 1995.

Qureshi, Regula Burckhardt. *Master Musicians of India: Hereditary Sarangi Players Speak*. New York: Routledge, 2007.

Stock, Jonathan P. J. *Musical Creativity in Twentieth-Century China: Abing, His Music, and Its Changing Meaning*. Rochester, NY: University of Rochester Press, 1996.

Vander, Judith. *Songprints:The Musical Experience of Five Shoshone Women*. Urbana: University of Illinois Press, 1988.

Vélez, Maria Teresa. *Drumming for the Gods: The Life and Times of Felipe Garcia Villamil*. Philadelphia: Temple University Press, 2000.

Chapter 7

Bithell, Carolyn. *Transported by Song: Corsican Voices from Oral Tradition to World Stage*. Lanham, MD: Scarecrow Press, 2007.

Buchanan, Donna. *Performing Democracy: Bulgarian Music and Musicians in Transition*. Chicago: University of Chicago Press, 2006.

Cooley, Timothy J. *Making Music in the Polish Tatras: Tourists, Ethnographers, and Mountain Musicians*. Bloomington: Indiana University Press, 2005.

DjeDje, Jacqueline Cogdell. *Fiddling in West Africa: Touching the Spirit in Fulbe, Hausa, and Dagbamba Cultures*. Bloomington: Indiana University Press, 2008.

Erlmann, Veit. *Music, Modernity, and the Global Imagination: South Africa and the West*. Oxford: Oxford University Press, 1999.

Rees, Helen. *Echoes of History: Naxi Music in Modern China*. New York: Oxford University Press, 2000.

Waterman, Christopher Alan. *Jùjú: A Social History and Ethnography of an African Popular Music*. Chicago: University of Chicago Press, 1990.
Weiss, Sarah. *Listening to an Earlier Java: Aesthetics, Gender, and the Music of Wayang in Central Java*. Seattle: University of Washington Press, 2007.

Chapter 8

Barz, Gregory, and Judah M. Cohen, eds. *The Culture of AIDS in Africa: Hope and Healing in Music and the Arts*. New York: Oxford University Press, 2011.
Greene, Paul D., and Thomas Porcello, eds. *Wired for Sound: Engineering and Technologies in Sonic Cultures*. Middletown, CT: Wesleyan University Press, 2005.
Horden, Peregrine, ed. *Music as Medicine: The History of Music Therapy since Antiquity*. Aldershot, UK: Ashgate, 2000.
Keyes, Cheryl L. *Rap Music and Street Consciousness*. Urbana: University of Illinois Press, 2002.
Pieslak, Jonathan. *Sound Targets: American Soldiers and Music in the Iraq War*. Bloomington: Indiana University Press, 2009.
Schloss, Joseph G. *Making Beats: The Art of Sample-Based Hip-Hop*. Middletown, CT: Wesleyan University Press, 2004.
Veal, Michael. E. *Dub: Soundscapes and Shattered Songs in Jamaican Reggae*. Middletown, CT: Wesleyan University Press, 2007.

Chapter 9

Schippers, Huib. *Facing the Music: Shaping Music Education from a Global Perspective*. Oxford: Oxford University Press, 2009.
Sheehy, Daniel. "A Few Notions about Philosophy and Strategy in Applied Ethnomusicology." *Ethnomusicology* 36, no. 3 (1992): 323–36.

Listening

Chapter 3

Lomax, Alan. *Afro-American Spirituals, Work Songs, and Ballads.* Rounder Records CD 1510 (1998).
Berliner, Paul. *The Soul of Mbira: Traditions of the Shona people of Rhodesia.* Nonesuch H-72054 (1973).
Berliner, Paul. *Zimbabwe: Shona Mbira Music* (orig. title: *Africa: Shona Mbira Music*). Nonesuch H-72077 (1977).
Schuyler, Philip. *Moroccan Folk Music.* Lyrichord 7229 (1972).
Schuyler, Philip. *Moroccan Sufi Music.* Lyrichord LP 7238.
Schuyler, Philip. *Moroccan Music: The Pan-Islamic Tradition.* Lyrichord 7240.
Schuyler, Philip. *Morocco: The Arabic Tradition in Moroccan Music.* EMI Odeon 3C 064–18264 (1977).
Yampolsky, Philip. *Music of Indonesia Series.* Smithsonian Folkways, 20 CDs (1991–1999).
The Solomon Islands, The Sounds of Bamboo: Instrumental Music of the 'Are'are People of Malaita. Multicultural Media MCM3007 (1997).
Navajo Songs. Smithsonian Folkways SFW40403 (1992).
Nusrat Fateh Ali Khan. *Sufi Qawwalis,* ARC Music Productions EUCD1737 (2002).
Boyd, Joe. *Balkana: Music of Bulgaria,* Hannibal HNCD 1335 (1987).
Central African Republic: Music of the Dendi, Nzakara, Banda Linda, Gbaya, Banda-dakpa, Ngbaka, Aka Pygmies. Auvidis D8020 (1989).

Chapter 4

The Rough Guide to Australian Aboriginal Music. World Music Network RGNET1207 (2008).

Boyd, Joe. *Balkanology: Ivo Papazov and His Orchestra.* Hannibal HNCD 1363 (1991).

Música Indígena: A Arte Vocal dos Suyá. São João Del Rei, Brazil: Tacape T-007 (1982).

Brésil—Candomblé De Angola—Afro-Brazilian Ritual Music. Inedit W260091 (1999).

Sacred Rhythms of Cuban Santería. Smithsonian Folkways SFW40419 (1995).

Rhythms of Rapture: Sacred Musics of Haitian Vodou. Smithsonian Folkways SFW40464 (1995).

Synchro Series: King Sunny Adé and his African Beats. Philadelphia: IndigeDisc ID0004 (2003).

Javanese Court Gamelan. Elektra Nonesuch 972044-2 (1991/1971).

Anthology of Indian Classical Music. Auvidis/UNESCO D8270 (1997).

Mountain Music of Peru. Vols. 1 and 2. Smithsonian Folkways SFW40020, 40406 (1991, 1994).

Chapter 5

Songs and Dances of the Flathead Indians. Folkways Records FW04445 (1953).

Albanian Intangible Heritage in CD: ISO—Polifonia & Monody. Uegen/UNESCO (2004).

Hugh Tracey, *Northern and Central Malawi: 1950, '57, and '58.* Stitching Sharp Wood Productions, International Library of African Music SWP014 (2000).

Chapter 6

Umm Kulthūm. *Oum Kalthoum: El sett (The Lady).* Buda Musique 82244-2 (2002).

The Best of Tito Puente, el rey del timbale! Rhino/BMG Special Productions R2 72817 (1997).

Tex Mex. ARC Music Productions EUCD1787 (2003).

Conjunto; Polkas de oro; Texas-Mexico Border Music. Vol. 5. Rounder Records CD6051 (1994).

Accordion Conjunto Champs of Tejano and Norteño Music, Arhoolie Records CD342 (2004).
The Mantaro Valley. Smithsonian Folkways SFW40467 (1995).

Chapter 7

Antologia del son de Mexico (Anthology of Mexican Sones). Corason COCD101; 102; 103 (1985).
Sinan Sakic and Juzni Vetar. *U Meni Potrazi Spas*, Juvekomerc PX JV-9412 (1994).
Münir Nurettin Beken, *The Art of the Turkish Ud*. Rounder Records (1997).
A. J. Racy and Simon Shaheen. *Taqāsīm: Art of Improvisation in Arab Music*. Lyrichord LYRCD 7374 (1993).
Marcel Cellier. *Le mystère des voix bulgare*. 2 vols. Nonesuch 79167, 79201 (1978, 1988).

Chapter 8

Paul Simon. *Graceland*. Warner Brothers 9 25447–2 (1986).
Paul Simon. *Rhythm of the Saints*. Warner Brothers 9 26098–2 (1990).
Sheila Chandra. *Weaving My Ancestors Voices*. Real World RW 24 (1992).
Apache Indian. *Make Way for the Indian*. Island ILPSD 8016 (1995).
Music of Indonesia. Vol. 2, *Indonesian Popular Music: Kroncong, Dangdut, and Langgam Jawa*. Smithsonian Folkways SFW40056 (1991).
The Orangemen of Ulster. Folkways Records FW03003 (1961).
The Music of Afghanistan. Rounder Select 82161–5121–2 (2003).
Nils-Aslak Valkeapää. *Goase Dusse (Loddesinfoniija/The Bird Symphony)*. DAT DC-15 (1994).
Co Co Li (i.e., Li Wen). *Di Da Di*. Sony Music Taiwan SDD 9801 489609–2 (1998).

Chapter 9

Avatar: Music from the Motion Picture. CD, Atlantic Records.
Avatar: Extended Collector's Edition. DVD, Twentieth-Century Fox Film Corporation.

Index

A

acoustemology, 110–11
acoustic ecology, 110
Adler, Guido, 16
aerophones, 19
aesthetics, 61–63
affinity groups, 28
Afghanistan, 109–10
African American music, 93
age, 71
agency, 50, 71–72, 81, 85
Aka music, 38, 46
al-Farabi, 13
al-Işbahānī, 13
Amiot, Jean Joseph Marie, 14
Anikulapo-Kuti, Fela, 81
anthropology, 21, 32, 56, 65
Apache Indian, 102
Apache music, 28
Arab music, 28, 36, 89, 94
Araujo, Samuel, 119
'Are'are music, 32–33, 67
Arom, Simha, 38,
art, definitions of, 60–61
Australia, 46
Autism Spectrum Disorder, 106
Avatar, 118
Aymara Indians, 54–55

B

Bach family, 69
bagpipe, Bulgarian, 36–37, 71
bajo sexto, 81
Bakan, Michael, 106
Balinese music, 103
Balkan music, 29
Bandambira, Mugayiwa, 30
Bartók, Béla, 15
Barz, Gregory, 107, 119
Becker, Judith, 51–52, 77–78, 95
Bella Coola Indians, 17
Berger, Harris, 84
Berliner Phongrammarchiv, 117
Berliner, Paul, 30, 38, 71
bhangra, 102
bi-musicality, 35–37
bird song, 5
Black music, 28
Blacking, John, 2, 5, 7, 23, 68, 114, 120
blues, 25, 93
Boethius, 12
Bohlman, Philip, 96
Bourdieu, Pierre, 50
bouzoukee, 20
Brazilian music, 28, 42, 103
Brinner, Benjamin, 85
Brown, James, 93
Bryant, Wanda, 118

Bulgarian music, 24, 29, 36–37, 46–47, 59–60, 71, 82–84, 99
Bureau of American Ethnology, 15
Burmese music, 103
Burney, Charles, 14

C

Cage, John, 5
Cameron, James, 118
Campbell, Patricia, 116
candomblé, 48
cantometrics, 52–54
Carnival, 28
Carter family, 69
Castelo-Branco, Salwa, 108
Central African Republic, 38
cents system, 18–19
Chandra, Sheila, 102
Charles, Ray, 93
Cheng, William, 105
Chinese music, 11–12, 88–90, 99, 103
chordophones, 19
Christianity and music, 91–92, 108
civil-rights movement, 25
class, 71, 85
Colombian music, 84, 118
colonialism, 13
comparative musicology, 16–17, 21
comparison, 3, 18–20, 21, 26
Confucius, 12
conjunto music, 81
Cooder, Ry, 101
Coplan, David, 97
Copper family, 69
copyright, 42
country music, 24
Croatia, 107
Cuban music, 72, 87, 91
cultural gray-out, 96, 120, 121
culture
  as cultural system, 56
  definition of, 65
  theories of, 85–87
culture-circle theory, 18

D

dance, 50, 66
dangdut, 105
Danielson, Virginia, 86
de la Rosa, Tony, 81
Deep Forest, 42, 101
Densmore, Frances, 15
Doubleday, Veronica, 110
dub, 24, 105

E

ecstasy. *See* trance
Egypt, 94
Ellis, Alexander John, 18–19
emic analysis, 32–33
emotion. *See* trance
England, 15
England, Nicholas, 22
Enlightenment, 14, 16
ethnicity, 71, 85
ethnology, 3, 15
Ethnomusicology, 20, 22
ethnomusicology
  definitions of, 1–10
  geographical perspectives on, 28
  themes in, 23
  as work, 113–21
ethno-pop, 8
ethnos, 3–4
ethnosonicology, 5
etic analysis, 32
Eurovision song context, 24
event description, 34–35
Ewe music, 28

F

Feld, Steven, 67, 100–101, 110
feminism, 25, 73
Ferris, William, 116
Fewkes, Walter, 17
fieldwork, 3, 27–44, 87
  AV recording during, 31–32, 37–40

choosing a site for, 27–30
documentation of, 37–40
ethics of, 30–31
learning music during, 31
as a method, 43
Flathead Indian music, 68–69
Fletcher, Alice Cunningham, 15
folk songs, 14
folklore, 14–15
folklorists, musical, 18
Folkways Records. *See* Smithsonian Folkways
Franklin, Aretha, 93
Friedson, Steven, 77
Frisbie, Charlotte, 33–34

G

Gabriel, Peter, 101
gagaku, 24
gaida. *See* bappipe, Bulgarian
gamelan, 24, 51–52, 105
Garfias, Robert, 39, 116
Geertz, Clifford, 56
gender, 30, 71, 73–75, 85
genius, 81
Georgia, Republic of, 40
Ghanaian music, 28, 39
globalization, 98–103
Goertzen, Chris, 72
gospel music, 25, 93
Grainger, Percy, 15
gray-out. *See* cultural gray-out
Greece, 11
Guthrie family, 69
Guy, Nancy, 112

H

Hagedorn, Katherine, 87
hardness scales, 22
harmony of the spheres, 11
heavy metal, 84
Hemetek, Ursula, 119
Herder, Johann Gottfried von, 14
Hindustani classical music, 24
hip-hop, 73, 105
historical ethnomusicology, 89
HIV/AIDS, 106–7, 119
Hood, Mantle, 22, 35, 39–40, 52
Hornbostel, Erich von, 117
Horner, James, 118
Hungary, 15

I

icon, 58–59
identity, 71–73
idiophones, 19
imperialism, 13
index, 58
Indian music, 28, 103
Indiana University, 20, 24
individual musicians, 78–87
Indonesian music, 36, 39
Institutional Review Boards, 31
intellectual property rights, 41–43
International Council for Traditional Music, 15
International Folk Music Council, 15
internet, 105
interviewing, 31–34
Islam and music, 6, 34–35, 67, 74, 94, 110
Israel, 96
Ivey, Bill, 116
Ivory Coast, 40

J

Jackson family, 69
Jamaican music, 24, 102, 105
Javanese music, 24, 36, 51–52, 85
jazz, 24–25, 71, 84
Jewish music, 28
joik, 111
Jones, Sir William, 13
jùjú, 50–51

K

Kaluli music, 67–68
Kant, Immanuel, 61–62
Keil, Charles, 105
Khan, Ustad Yunnus Husain, 55
Kingsbury, Henry, 56
Kishibe, Shigeo, 20
Kodály, Zoltán, 15
Koen, Benjamin, 106
Kolinski, Mieczyslaw, 21
Korean music, 40
Kosovo, 108
Kulthūm, Umm, 81, 86
Kunst, Jaap, 3, 7, 20, 35

L

Lakota music, 15
Lam, Joseph, 88
Lévi-Strauss, Claude, 51
Lomax, Alan, 38, 52–54, 96
Lomax, John, 38
Lomax Hawes, Bess, 116, 119
Longoria, Valerio, 81
Lysloff, René, 104

M

Macedonia, 74
Maestre, Jaime, 118
Malawi, 76–77
Mall of America, music in, 24
Manuel, Peter, 72, 95
Martinez, Narcisco, 81
Marxism, 95
mbira dzavadzimu, 30
McAllester, David, 20, 33–34, 63
medical ethnomusicology, 107
Meintjes, Louise, 101–2, 105
melograph, 40
membranophones, 19
Merriam, Alan, 3, 20, 22–24, 48, 65–66, 68, 114
metaphor, 44–64
Mexican music, 28, 91
Milošević, Slobodan, 94
Mitchell, Frank, 33
Miyagi Michio, 99
modernization, 92, 96, 99
Moisala, Pirrko, 30
monogenesis, 17
mousikē, 4–8
Mozart family, 69
multiculturalism, 25
music
  of affinity groups, 28
  as art, 60–64
  and climate change, 110–12
  in clubs, bars, prisons, 28
  communication in, 47–48
  conservatories of, 95
  and crying, 49–50
  as cultural form, 51–56
  as or in culture, 3, 21–22, 25, 65–78
  definitions of, 4–8
  distribution of, 17
  as entertainment, 49
  ethics of, 13
  history of, 88–97
  and identity, 71–73
  learning of, 68–71
  lessons in, 69
  local concepts of, 66–68
  nature of, 44–64
  as a resource, 45–51
  as social behavior, 51–56
  as a system of signs, 57–59
  and technology, 103–6
  as text, 56–57
  theory of, 32
  and war, 107–10
  universals in, 4, 17
musical analysis, 38, 40–41, 62
musical instruments, 19–20

musicality, 1
musicking, 6
musicology, 3, 8, 16, 21, 82
Musikwissenschaft, 16

N

nationalism, 15, 87
Native American music, 14–15, 24
Navajo music, 33, 63
Neher, Andrew, 76
Nettl, Bruno, 21, 97
ngoma, 6
Nigerian music, 50–55
Nketia, J. H. Kwabena, 23
non-Western music, 7
norteño, 24
North Indian classical music, 54
Northern Ireland, 108–9

O

Occaneechi Indians, 72–73
occupation, 71
O'Connell, John, 108
oral history, 31, 33–34

P

Pakistan, 34–35
Papua New Guinea, 68
participant-observation, 31, 34–35
Peirce, C. S., 58
Peña, Manuel, 81
Pettan, Svanibor, 108, 119
Philippines, 39
phonograph, 16, 117
Plato, 12
politics of identity, 25
polygenesis, 18
popular music, 98–103
possession. *See* trance
practice theory, 50, 86
primitive music, 17
Pueblo Indians, 51
Puente, Tito, 81
Puerto Rican music, 24, 72
Pythagoras, 11, 19

Q

Qawwali music, 34–35
Qur'anic chant, 36
Qureshi, Regula, 34–35

R

race, 71, 85
Racy, A.J., 94
Rajasthani music, 28
Ramnarine, Tina, 111
rap, 24–25
Rasmussen, Anne, 36
Rasmussen, Ljerka, 93
recordings, audio, 37–41
reggae, 24, 102
Revista musical chilena, 20
Rhodes, Willard, 20
Rimsky-Korsakov, Nikolay, 15
rock, 73, 84
Romero, Raúl, 86
Rouget, Gilbert, 76–77
Rousseau, Jean-Jacques, 14
Russia, 15

S

Sachs, Curt, 19
Sachs-Hornbostel system, 19–20
Saint Augustine, 12
Sakata, Hiromi Lorraine, 37
salsa, 24, 72
samba, 28
Sámi music, 111
santería, 48, 87
sarangi, 54

Sawa, George, 89
Schafer, R. Murray, 110
Schuyler, Philip, 39
Seeger family, 69
Seeger, Anthony, 42–43, 47, 69–70, 108, 117, 119–20
Seeger, Charles, 20, 40
semiotics, 57–58
Serbian music, 24
Shanghai music, 28
Sharp, Cecil, 15
Sheehy, Daniel, 116, 118–19
Shelemay, Kay Kaufman, 37
Shona music, 30, 76
Simon, Paul, 101–2
Small, Christopher, 6
Smithsonian Folklife Festival, 117
Smithsonian Folkways, 39
Smithsonian Institution, 116
Society for Ethnomusicology, 9, 20, 24, 114
Society for Research on Asiatic Music, 20
Solomon Islands, 32, 40
son, of Cuba and Mexico, 91
sonograph, 40
soul music, 25
sound studies, 5, 110
South Africa, 68, 101, 105
Spencer, Herbert, 17
Stokes, Martin, 114
structural functionalism, 45
structuralism, 51
subculture, 4
Sufism and music, 34–35, 67
Sugarman, Jane, 75
Suyá music, 42, 47, 69–70, 109
Sweers, Britta, 119
Switzerland, 40
syncretism, 91

T

tabla, 54
Taiwanese music, 112
Tajikistan, 106
talent, 1, 69, 79
Taylor, Timothy, 102
technoculture, 104
Tenzer, Michael, 62
Tex-Mex music, 81
Thai music, 28
Tibetan music, 103
Timbuka music, 76–77
Titon, Jeff Todd, 6, 43
traditional music, 7
trance, 75–78
transcription, 14, 22, 40–41
turbofolk, 24, 94
Turino, Thomas, 55, 58–59, 63
Turkish music, 40, 94, 103

U

UCLA. *See* University of California, Los Angeles
Ulfah, Ibu Maria, 36
Universals. *See* music, universals in
University of California, Los Angeles, 20, 40
University of Illinois, 20

V

Valkeapää, Nils-Aslak, 111
Van Buren, Katherine, 119
Varimezov, Kostadin, 82–83
Varimezova, Todora, 67, 82
Vaughan Williams, Ralph, 15
Venda music, 68
Vienna Phongrammarchiv, 117
Villareal, Alberto, 87
vodoun, 48

W

Waterman, Christopher, 24, 46, 50
Waxer, Lise, 84

whale song, 5
White, Leslie, 51

Y

Yampolsky, Philip, 39
Yirkalla music, 46
Yugoslav music,
93–94

Z

Zemp, Hugo, 32–33, 40, 42
Zimbabwe, 30